DEMOCRATIZING OUR DATA

DEMOCRATIZING OUR DATA

A Manifesto

JULIA LANE

The MIT Press
Cambridge, Massachusetts
London, England

This book was set in Adobe Garamond and Berthold Akzidenz Grotesk by Jen Jackowitz. Printed and bound in the United States of America.

Library of Congress Cataloging-in-Publication Data

Names: Lane, Julia I., author.
Title: Democratizing our data : a manifesto / Julia Lane.
Description: Cambridge, Massachusetts : The MIT Press, [2020] | Includes
  bibliographical references and index.
Identifiers: LCCN 2019057265 | ISBN 9780262044325 (hardcover)
Subjects: LCSH: United States--Statistical services--Standards. |
  Statistical decision--Standards. | Quantitative research--Standards.
Classification: LCC HA37.U55 L34 2020 | DDC 352.7/50973--dc23
LC record available at https://lccn.loc.gov/2019057265

10 9 8 7 6 5 4 3 2 1

The Coleridge Initiative team:
Past, Present, and Future

Contents

Preface *ix*

1 **THE PROBLEM, WHY IT MATTERS, AND WHAT TO DO** *1*

2 **THE CURRENT STATE OF PLAY** *19*

3 **SET UP TO FAIL** *41*

4 **A SUCCESSFUL MODEL** *63*

5 **SETTING UP FOR SUCCESS** *83*

6 **ESTABLISHING THE FOUNDATION** *107*

7 **THE FUTURE** *121*

Notes *143*

Index *167*

Preface

Not long ago I had lunch with one of the top statisticians in the country, who looked across the table and said, "The information needs of people making important decisions are changing so rapidly. It's difficult for the federal government to meet those needs—the system is not designed for rapid change. We need to rethink how people can get consistently high-quality information when they need it from a trustworthy source. Our future depends on it." Another former government statistician put it more succinctly: "The federal system is broken, and I don't know if anything can fix it. So many good people, and nothing ever changes." A colleague who has spent over thirty years working within the system believes the problem is that even when senior management knows what to do, there is no incentive to take big risks and rock the boat, so the safest thing for both managers and frontline staff is to continue doing what they have always done and make very small incremental changes. And that does not meet today's needs.

Think of the massive impact of the coronavirus on jobs and society in 2020. Governments at all levels urgently needed numbers that could tell them how many jobs were lost and how the most vulnerable in society were affected; the infrastructure was not there.

This book is intended to drive change in the system that the United States uses to produce public statistics. It is not a call for more funding, although lack of funding has contributed to the current crisis. It is a call to fundamentally reorganize data production.

The reasons are clear. Access to high-quality information to make good decisions is necessary for society to function. Reliable, accurate, timely information levels the playing field for businesses and individuals alike. It is necessary at every level of our economy and society—to help small businesses succeed, schools serve parents and students, central banks make sound policy, and people make major life decisions.

The need for change is also clear. Costs to collect information through traditional means continue to increase, and response rates to government surveys continue to decrease. Government-produced data should accurately represent American economic and social activity, and our current system is badly strained and at high risk of future failure. Our democracy is threatened without timely, relevant data and evidence that reflects our economy and society, and we should be outraged that our system has fallen behind. This book is a wake-up call for Americans to understand how our data are used to create important information underlying major decisions that affect our lives every day, why the current system is breaking, and the immediate steps necessary to fix it.

The path outlined in the book is the result of over twenty-five years of experience working with data in academia, many levels of government, and the private sector. Of course, no one can possibly understand the workings of the entire system, but I stand on the shoulders of the writings of many giants, not least of whom is Janet Norwood, a noted economist and statistician who headed the US Bureau of Labor Statistics for thirteen years.

This is the time to effect change. There are new data, new tools, and new technologies that can be combined in new ways to create new evidence. There are enough people of good will with enough determination to get things done. Recent legislation has created an opportunity to rethink the organizational data infrastructure. New legislation could take advantage of this golden moment and truly democratize our data.

The time is now.

Like any author, I owe enormous debts to the many colleagues with whom I have worked over the years. I have been privileged to work with incredibly dedicated and visionary colleagues at New York University's Coleridge Initiative, and our associated university and agency partners. I am incredibly grateful to all the staff in the federal statistical system and in programmatic agencies at the federal, state, and local government levels who work hard to make a difference, often against daunting odds. I name just a few in the book, but literally hundreds of people contributed to the LEHD (Longitudinal Employer–Household Dynamics) program, to IRIS (Institute for Research on Innovation and Science) at the University of Michigan, and to the Coleridge Initiative. I am indebted to all of them.

The philanthropic foundations, particularly Schmidt Futures, the Alfred P. Sloan Foundation, the Overdeck Family Foundation, and the Bill and Melinda Gates Foundation, have been game changers in placing their trust in the work that we have been doing and enabling us to demonstrate what can be done.

My developmental editor David Weinberger helped shape and reshape this book with constant good humor and wise suggestions. Ian Glennon provided the initial research, particularly for chapter 2. Jason Owen Smith and Nancy Calvin-Naylor provided very useful comments on chapter 4. Paco Nathan, Jonathan Morgan, Ian Mulvany, and Drew Gordon were extremely influential in the discussion of automation in chapter 5. Stefan Bender, Nick Greenia, Frauke Kreuter, Nancy Potok, Bryant Renaud, and Brock Webb provided valuable suggestions and input at all stages of the manuscript. Mike Holland provided great assistance in reviewing the entire book, particularly in the discussion of federally funded research and development centers in chapter 7. All remaining errors are, of course, my own.

My MIT Press editor, Emily Taber, has provided an unbelievable amount of support and guidance—well beyond anything I deserved.

Finally, I owe my greatest debt to my husband, Dennis Glennon, who has put up with me during this process—and for many years before that!

1 THE PROBLEM, WHY IT MATTERS, AND WHAT TO DO

Public data are foundational to our democratic system. We know about income inequality and job trends thanks to data from the Bureau of Labor Statistics. We know what's happening to economic growth thanks to data from the US Census Bureau. We know about the impact of business tax changes thanks to data from the Statistics of Income Division. Data like these are profoundly important for most of us, and especially for individuals and small businesses who can't pay for expensive experts to produce customized reports.

One of government's jobs is to level the data playing field. Statistical agencies have historically been the source of accurate and objective information for democracies, due to the limitations of private sector–produced data. For example, emergency supplies probably shouldn't be allocated to an area based on the frequency of tweets from that location. Why? Because that would mean more supplies going to the people who tweet, underserving babies and elderly residents who are less likely to have Twitter accounts. Emergency supplies should be allocated based on information about the people likely to need such supplies, and government data are the way in which we ensure that the right people are counted. If people aren't counted, they don't count, and that threatens our democracy.

But recently, the playing field has been tilting against public data. Our current statistical system is under stress, too often based on old technology and with too little room for innovation. Our public statistical institutions often are not structurally capable of taking advantage of massive changes in the availability of data and the public need for new and better data to make decisions. And without breakthroughs in public measurement, we're not going to get intelligent public decision-making.[1] Over twenty years ago, one of the great statistical administrators of the twentieth century, Janet Norwood, pointed to the failing organizational structure of federal statistics and warned that, "In a democratic society, public policy choices can be made intelligently only when the people making the decisions can rely on accurate and objective statistical information to inform them of the choices they face and the results of choices they make."[2]

We must rethink ways to democratize data. There are successful models to follow and new legislation that can help effect change. The private sector's Data Revolution—where new types of data are collected and new measurements created by the private sector to build machine learning and artificial intelligence algorithms—can be mirrored by a public sector Data Revolution, one that is characterized by attention to counting all who should be counted, measuring what should be measured, and protecting privacy and confidentiality. Just as US private sector companies—Google, Amazon, Microsoft, Apple, and Facebook—have led the world in the use of data for profit, the US can show the world how to produce data for the public good.

There are massive challenges to be addressed. The national statistical system—our national system of measurement—has ossified. Public agencies struggle to change the approach to collecting the statistics that they have produced for decades—in some cases, as we shall see, since the Great Depression. Hamstrung by excessive legislative control, inertia, lack of incentives, ill-advised budget cuts, and the "tyranny of the established," they have largely lost the ability to innovate or respond to quickly changing user needs.[3] Despite massive increases in the availability of new types of data, such as administrative records (data produced through the administration of government programs, such as tax records) or by digital activities (such as social media or cell phone calls), the US statistical agencies struggle to operationalize their use.[4] Worse still, the government agencies that produce public data are at the bottom of the funding chain—staffing is being cut, funding is stagnant if not being outright slashed, and entire agencies are being decimated.[5]

If we don't move quickly, the cuts that have already affected physical, research, and education infrastructures[6] will also eventually destroy our public data infrastructure and threaten our democracy. Trust in government institutions will be eroded if government actions are based on political preference rather than grounded in statistics. The fairness of legislation will be questioned if there is not impartial data whereby the public can examine the impact of legislative changes in, for example, the provision of health care and the imposition of taxes. National problems, like the opioid crisis, will not be addressed, because governments won't know where or how to allocate resources. Lack of access to public data will increase the power of big businesses, which can pay for data to make better decisions, and reduce the power of small businesses, which can't. The list is endless because the needs are endless.

This book provides a solution to the impending critical failure in public data. Our current approach and the current budget realities mean that we cannot produce all the statistics needed to meet today's expectations for informing increasingly complex public decisions. We must design a new statistical system that will produce public data that are useful at all levels of government—and make scientific, careful, and responsible use of many newly available data, such as administrative records from agencies that administer government programs, data generated from the digital lives of citizens, and even data generated within the private sector.

This book will paint a picture of what this new system could look like, focusing on the innovations necessary to disrupt the existing federal statistical system, with the goal of providing useful and timely data from trusted sources so that we, the people, have the information necessary to make better decisions.

WHY IT MATTERS

Measurement is at the core of democracy, as Simon Winchester points out: "All life depends to some extent on measurement, and in the very earliest days of social organization a clear indication of advancement and sophistication was the degree to which systems of measurement had been established, codified, agreed to and employed."[7] Yet public data and measurement have to be paid for out of the public purse, so there is great scrutiny of costs and quality. The challenge public agencies face is that, as

Erik Brynjolffson, the director of MIT's Initiative on the Digital Economy, points out, we have become used to getting digital goods that are free . . . and instant and useful. Yet in a world where private data are getting cheaper, the current system of producing public data costs a lot of money—and costs are going up, not down. One standard is how much it costs the Census Bureau to count the US population. In 2018 dollars, the 1960 Census cost about $1 billion, or about $5.50 per person. The 1990 Census cost about $20 per head.[8] The 2020 Census is projected to cost about $16 billion, or about $48 per head.[9] And the process is far from instant: Census Day is April 1, 2020, but the results won't be delivered until December.

Another standard is the quality of data that are collected. Take a look, for example, at the National Center for Health Statistics report to the Council of Professional Associations on Federal Statistics.[10] Response rates on the National Health Interview Survey have dropped by over 20 percentage points, increasing the risk of nonresponse bias, and the rate at which respondents "break off" or fail to complete the survey has almost tripled over a twenty-year period.

As a result, communities are not getting all the information they need from government for decision-making. If we made a checklist of features of data systems that have made private sector businesses like Amazon and Google successful, it might include producing data that are: (1) real-time so customers can make quick decisions; (2) accurate so customers aren't misled; (3) complete so there is enough information for the customer to make a decision; (4) relevant to the customer; (5) accessible so the customer can easily get to information and use it; (6) interpretable so everyone can understand what the data mean;

(7) innovative so customers have access to new products; and (8) granular enough so each customer has customized information.

If we were to look at the flagship programs of the federal system, they don't have those traits. Take, for example, the national government's largest survey—the Census Bureau's *American Community Survey* (ACS). It was originally designed to consistently measure the entire country so that national programs that allocated dollars to communities based on various characteristics were comparing the whole country on the same basis. It is an enormous and expensive household survey. It asks questions of 295,000 households every month—3.5 million individuals a year. The cost to the Census Bureau is about $220 million[11] and another $64 million can be attributed to the respondents in the value of the time taken to answer the questions.[12] Because there is no high-quality alternative, it is used in hundreds if not thousands of local decisions—as the ACS website says, it "helps local officials, community leaders, and businesses understand the changes taking place in their communities."[13] In New York alone, the police department must report on priority areas that are determined, in part, using ACS poverty measures,[14] pharmacies must provide translations for top languages as defined by the ACS,[15] and the New York Department of Education took 2008 ACS population estimates[16] into account when it decided to make Diwali a school holiday.

Yet while reliable local data are desperately needed, the very expensive ACS data are too error prone for reliable local decision-making. The reasons for this include the survey design, sample sizes that are too small, public interpretation of margins of error when sample sizes are small, and lack of timely dissemination of data.

I'll discuss some of the details of these reasons in chapter 2—but one core problem is the reliance on old technology. The data are collected by means of mailing a survey to a random set of households (one out of 480 households in any given month). One person is asked to fill out the survey on behalf of everyone else in the household, as well as to answer questions about the housing unit itself. To give you a sense of the issues with this approach: there is no complete national list of households (the Census Bureau's list misses about 6 percent of households), about a third of recipients refuse to respond, and of those who respond, many do not fill out all parts of the survey.[17] There is follow-up of a subset of nonresponders by phone, internet, and in-person interviews, but each one of these introduces different sources of bias in terms of who responds and how they respond. Because response rates vary by geography and demography, those biases can be very difficult to adjust for.[18] Such problems are not unique to the ACS; surveys in general are less and less likely to be truly representative of the people in the United States and the mismatch between intentions and reality can result in the systematic erasure of millions of Americans from governmental decision-making.

Statistical agencies face major privacy challenges as well. The increased availability of data on the internet means that it is much easier to reidentify survey respondents, so more and more noise has to be introduced into the data in order to protect respondent privacy. This noise results in reduced data reliability, particularly for small populations.[19] For example, the Census Bureau is systematically making data worse to protect privacy.

> Census data from 2010 showed that a single Asian couple—a 63-year-old man and a 58-year-old woman—lived on Liberty Island, at the base of the Statue of Liberty. That was news to

David Luchsinger, who had taken the job as the superintendent for the national monument the year before. On Census Day in 2010, Mr. Luchsinger was 59, and his wife, Debra, was 49. In an interview, they said they had identified as white on the questionnaire, and they were the island's real occupants.

Before releasing its data, the Census Bureau had "swapped" the Luchsingers with another household living in another part of the state, who matched them on some key questions. This mechanism preserved their privacy, and kept summaries like the voting age population of the island correct, but also introduced some uncertainty into the data.[20]

Yes, you read that right. Not only are US taxpayers paying $48 a head to be counted (not including the cost of taxpayer time to fill out the forms), but then the numbers are systematically distorted and made less useful to protect privacy. Community input into the tradeoff between data quality and privacy protection is sorely needed.

In addition, the data that are produced are hard to interpret and apply at the state or local level. The ACS has come under fire for the fact that the estimates the survey produces are "simply too imprecise for small area geography."[21]

What is the practical implication? Take the measurement of child poverty, for example, which is used by state and local governments to figure out how to allocate taxpayer dollars to poor children. In one county (Autauga) in Alabama, with a total population of about fifty-five thousand, the ACS estimates that 139 children under age 5 live in poverty—plus or minus 178! So the plausible range is somewhere between 0 and 317.[22]

The problem is not just that the errors are large, but also that they are larger, reflecting lower-quality estimates, for lower-income and central city neighborhoods[23]—precisely the areas that are often targeted for policy interventions. This undemocratic distortion of millions of Americans will result in the inaccurate estimation of, for example, the effects of health and tax policy on low-income individuals, and, unfortunately, the inequality in data coverage is increasing.

Even worse, the data are not timely. They are made available two years after they are collected (in May of 2019, 2017 data are available on the ACS website) and the five-year rolling average approach (aggregating over a moving window of the previous five years of data as the survey date rolls through time) means that the 2017 data include survey information from 2013. Obviously, the information is largely unsuitable for areas that are rapidly changing due to immigration, outmigration, or the opening or closure of major employers.

What to Do

Because the system the federal government uses to produce statistical data is large and complex, a number of systemic changes need to be made. The organizational structure, as well as the composition and skill of the government workforce, needs to change. And the ties to community and local demand need to be institutionalized and made stronger.

The details will be discussed later in the book, but simply put, the government structure has to change so that innovation can occur and new data can be produced. In the private sector, new businesses are born and expand, replacing older businesses and providing new services. For example, firms like Waze figured out how to combine and analyze massive amounts of information about individual car trips in order to provide instant information to travelers about the best way to get from A to B. Their business, and others like them, replaced the business of producing physical maps that were difficult to use and often out of date.

Since that solution doesn't work for governments, we need to identify what parts of the federal statistical system should be retained and what parts should be reallocated. The challenge is identifying an alternative. An important argument in this book is that the Data Revolution makes it possible.

Changing the workforce is critical. For data to have value, the employees in an organization have to have the skills necessary to translate that data into information. The entire structure of the private sector has been transformed in the past twenty years to reflect the need for such skills. In 2018, one of the biggest US companies, Facebook, grounded in data, had a market value per employee of about $20.5 million, with very little physical capital and a workforce skilled in manipulating data. Twenty years ago, one of the biggest US companies, General Motors, grounded in manufacturing, had a market value of $230,000 per employee, with a great deal of physical capital and a skilled manufacturing workforce.[24] Such change is difficult to effect in the public sector. Government salary structures make it difficult to hire and retain enough in-house data analysts, let alone respond quickly to reward employees for acquiring new skills. The government is competing against Facebook and Google not only for salaries but also prestige. The occupational classification of "data scientist" didn't even exist in the federal government until June of 2019.[25] Open source tools, like Python, which are commonly used in private-sector data analysis, are regarded with suspicion by many government IT organizations. The pressures to meet existing program needs make it difficult for agency staff to try something new, and while failure is celebrated in the private sector, it can be career ending in the public sector. These combined challenges have led to the current situation—agencies cannot get the significant resources necessary to make use of new data, and because they don't use new data, they don't get new resources.

New products that respond to community needs must be developed. There is a huge opportunity to do so. The amount of new data available is overwhelming.[26] Real-time data can be collected on cell phones, from social media sites, as a result of retail transactions, and by sensors or simply driving your car. Turning the data into useable information requires a very different set of skills than the ones deployed in the survey world. Data need to be gathered, prepared, transformed, cleaned, and explored, using different tools. The results need to be stored using new database tools, and analyzed using new techniques like machine learning and network analysis. Visualization and computational techniques are fundamentally different with data on a massive scale, rather than simply tens of thousands of survey answers. The privacy issues are different, as are the requirements for data search and discovery and reproducibility.[27]

While today's data world is, in many ways, a Wild West, data being produced for the public sector need to be designed carefully. The key elements of the federal statistical infrastructure are too important to lose: we need to expand the current statistical system to think about how public data should be produced, and how they must be trustworthy and measured well and consistently over time, and how confidential information should be protected. A world in which all data are produced by a market-driven private sector could be a dangerous one—where there are many unidentified or unreported biases; where privacy is not protected; where national statistics could be altered for the right price; where if a business changes its data collection approach, the unemployment numbers could skyrocket (or drop); where respondents' information could be sold to the highest bidder.[28]

Action is required because the way governments produce statistics won't change by itself. In the private sector, market forces create the impetus for change, because organizations that don't adapt are driven out of business. There's no similar force driving government change. Over the past thirty years, I've worked with people at all levels of government—federal, state, county, and city—in the United States and throughout the world. I've developed tremendous respect and admiration for the highly skilled and dedicated workforce that brings us the information driving our economy. These professionals know what needs to be done to make change happen. Hundreds of studies have provided useful recommendations. But when, in the course of thirty years, hundreds of good people try to change the system and the system doesn't change, it's clear nothing is going to happen without disruption.

This book proposes a new and, yes, disruptive approach that spells out what to do. It keeps the best elements of the current model—the trust, professionalism, and continuity—while taking away the worst elements—the bureaucracy and rigidity. It proposes a restructuring to create a system that will:

1. Produce public statistics that are useful at all levels—federal, state, and local.
2. Empower a government workforce to innovate in response to new needs.

3. Create a trusted organization that is incentivized to respond to community demand.

This is a golden moment to rethink data use by establishing, codifying, agreeing to, and employing new systems of measurement. Governments at the state and local levels are upping their investment in developing analytics teams to support better management. At the federal level, Congress passed the Foundations for Evidence-Based Policymaking Act of 2018 and the White House published the first Federal Data Strategy. Both efforts require agencies to invest in data, analytical approaches, and more thorough evaluation activities to get rid of programs that don't work and expand programs that do. Many state and local governments are turning to data- and evidence-driven decision-making and forming new partnerships with universities, with the private sector, and with each other to do so.

The challenge is making sure that the focus is on creating new value rather than creating new processes. In the private sector, thousands of firms get started; only the successful ones survive. Federal, state, and local governments don't have the pressure of failure, so their response is to establish new positions. The federal government's response has been to require each of the twenty-four major US government agencies to have a chief data officer (CDO), a chief evaluation officer, and a senior statistical officer; at last count, nearly fifty states, counties, and cities had also hired CDOs. Ensuring that the people in these positions have the support or control that they need to succeed is essential: if an ineffective system is introduced in government, it can be hard to course-correct. Governments at all levels are investing in training their staff to acquire data skills; it will be similarly critical to ensure those investments are substantive rather than perfunctory.

Chapter 2 goes into the details of how key indicators of factors such as economic activity are measured, and why measurement is so difficult. The current system was designed to be great at counting guns and butter for World War II supplies. But although manufacturing and agriculture are much less important now than they were a century ago, the government continues to be much better at counting manufacturing output (648 industry categories) than finance and insurance output (89 industry categories).[29] Why? It's like the old story of a drunk looking for his lost keys under a streetlight. A policeman stops to help, and after a fruitless search, the policeman asks if the keys were really lost there. The drunk says, no—he lost them in the alley. The policeman, of course, asks the drunk why he isn't looking in the alley, and the drunk answers, "This is where the light is." That's government. The public sector continues to look under the streetlight because it's so difficult to change.

We'll highlight the issues by discussing how people work and generate products and why governments need to rethink how and what they measure and why they measure it.[30] We'll start by talking about one of the most important measures that government produces—gross domestic product, or GDP, which is the international measure of economic activity in each country. GDP is sometimes also used to measure economic well-being, but as we'll see later on, it is not designed for that, so it doesn't measure it very well. Digital technologies have fundamentally changed the way in which business is done and people interact.[31] This leads to huge and important questions about how to measure twenty-first-century activity.[32] How should "free" search or online services be valued when the exchange is not money, but information? How should smartphone apps be valued? How should investment in research be valued? How should quality increases be valued?

We will also talk about why measurement is so difficult. We'll go into the issues in more detail in chapter 2, but the challenge is that much of the new types of data capture observed behavior but don't provide the understanding of how the data are generated, making measurement difficult. For example, if data from a state Department of Labor show that someone doesn't have a job, that person might not be unemployed—he or she might be in school, in jail, on welfare, retired, or caring for a child. Knowing the cause is important for understanding what is being measured. Or, if data from a credit card company show that sales are up (or down) in a particular city, it might be because that company has gained (or lost) customers.[33] The skills necessary to turn the data into information are also not common—the data are messy, with very little information about their strengths and weaknesses. As an example of messiness, when employers report employee counts from their human resource records to their state Department of Labor and the data are aggregated to count the number of jobs in each state, some individuals show up with hundreds of employers in a given quarter. It may be that those individuals are extremely busy—or it may be that a social security number is being shared!

The takeaway from chapter 2 is that economic and social measurement is difficult—and that statistical agencies are not structured to innovate and develop new and better measures in response to a changing world.

Chapter 3 describes why statistical measurement and innovation are so difficult in the United States. The structure of the federal statistical system is a major factor. It is unusually fragmented—there are thirteen major statistical agencies and approximately one hundred minor data collection entities scattered throughout the government. The chapter also describes the best aspects of the current system—trust, professionalism, and continuity. As one would expect, a major value of the federal statistical system is that there are rules, there are agencies and legal frameworks that enforce the rules, and the rules are well known. There are huge benefits to this approach—consistency, resistance to outside influence, and independence. But I will also argue that the slowness and lack of innovation are crippling public data and measurement—and the organizational structure does not augur well for the possibility of change.

Chapter 4 describes how new approaches to collecting and combining data can emerge as a result of changing demand and the actions of an engaged and interested community. This chapter also sets the stage for thinking about the qualities that a new federal data system must embody, which are then discussed in further detail in the last three chapters of the book.

Chapter 5 walks through what it will take to build a new system—how to create value while at the same time protecting privacy. It proposes the use of new technologies and a more automated, transparent, and accountable framework for creating high-quality data. It is inspired by the success of private sector companies like TripAdvisor and Amazon—where high-value data products are created, tested, and produced—and also informed by the privacy and quality concerns raised by these successes.

Of course, a key feature of this new system is an approach to inspiring civil servants and creating and empowering an engaged and innovative workforce. That is the focus of chapter 6, where I draw on my experiences working with federal, state, and local agencies.

The last chapter proposes a new organizational model that is inspired by institutional success in other areas. This new model has the potential to transform the world of measurement and statistics in a way that democratizes both access and use.

Failure to act could threaten our democratic infrastructure. The slow decline in data quality combined with increasing costs could well lead budget-conscious legislatures to simply save money by shutting down parts of the statistical system. We must begin the process of careful restructuring now—while we can—so that all Americans will be fairly represented when our democratic institutions are charged with making evidence-based decisions. As Janet Norwood said, this is essential so that the people making these decisions "can rely on accurate and objective statistical information to inform them of the choices they face and the results of choices they make."[34]

We need to build a new public data infrastructure that democratizes data.

2 THE CURRENT STATE OF PLAY

The problems of our public measurement system are perhaps best illustrated by detailing the problems of one of our best-known national statistics—gross domestic product—which counts the market value of all final goods (in other words, the finished products: paper, not timber) and services produced within a country in a given period of time. When analysts talk about the strength of the American economy, or national income accounts, they are often talking about our GDP. However, the imperfections of GDP are well known, and have been well known for a very long time. It has been referred to as a "Frankenstein's monster" and an "arbitrary, oversimplified human invention that we slavishly follow" . . . a modern "cult."[1] Sadly, this is not a new revelation. Paraphrasing an eloquent speech by presidential candidate Robert F. Kennedy in 1968: "We judge the United States by production—we count air pollution, cigarette advertising, locks for our doors and jails for people who break them. We count the destruction of the redwood, the production of nuclear warheads, but not the health of our children, the beauty of poetry, the intelligence of our public debate or the integrity of our officials. . . . It measures everything in short, except that which makes life worthwhile."[2]

Ouch.

But the GDP measure is not the only flawed measure—it is only illustrative. Another well-known set of statistics used to describe the strength of the economy is for the levels of unemployment and employment, and there is a parallel set of problems associated with these as well. The most well-known measure is drawn from the Current Population Survey that surveys about 60,000 households every month to find out people's employment status. The reports of the results, which are issued by the Bureau of Labor Statistics on the first Friday of every month with great fanfare, can change government policies and the direction of markets. Election campaigns are often won or lost on the basis of employment statistics. The problem is that the jobs numbers are increasingly incomplete, both because of the development of the gig economy[3] and because the survey is missing more and more people at both ends (or margins) of the income distribution.[4] In the careful language of economists, this leads to undercounting the employment status of such marginal individuals "even though marginal workers and marginal jobs are the most sensitive to changing labor market conditions."[5]

So the official data don't fully measure either the degree to which important swaths of the workforce are marginalized or their vulnerability to economic shocks. It has been argued that the 2016 presidential election results were directly a result of Democrats not fully understanding the disproportionately negative effect of shocks like the North American Free Trade Agreement and immigration on income inequality and working-class voters.

The problem is not that the measures have serious flaws. That is old news to economists. The economy is complex, and any attempt to measure it will fall short in some way. The problem is that the measurement structure was designed a very long time ago, and is not getting better with more understanding and more data; in fact, it's getting worse. The bigger questions are why do government agencies continue to produce GDP and employment measures the way that they always have, and why are they so slow to change? There are three main reasons.

The first is that the agencies have a difficult task—they have to produce one number that summarizes incredibly complex economic phenomena. The idea of measuring the health of the economy with a single number is a powerful one, and a single measure does have some value. Indeed, the precursor to the modern GDP measure had enormous value when it was invented more than eighty years ago to show the magnitude of the Great Depression. By showing that economic output had been cut in half in just three years, it provided the evidence of the need for the New Deal and later the data to organize the war effort. That single measure contributed to "liberating the United States from the tyranny of economic ignorance," says Dirk Philipsen in his 2015 book, *The Little Big Number: How GDP Came to Rule the World and What to Do About It.*[6] Nowadays GDP is used by the World Bank as a criterion for loans, and by the European Union for membership. Similarly, summary employment levels provide simple targets for national policy makers to aim for and they are easily understood measures. As a result, government agencies receive funding from Congress to produce these well-understood and well-known targets and it is very hard to change funding lines.

The second reason is that, while there is a common understanding that these are imperfect statistics and that we need new measures,[7] it is difficult to change.

In the case of GDP, the counting apparatus maintains institutional biases from when it was first developed to respond to a pair of cataclysms in the middle of the last century: it is essentially an international accounting exercise that is designed to count what is bought by consumers and businesses and what is spent by governments, so it measures the price that is paid for the goods and services produced by the economy.[8] Perhaps unsurprisingly for a measure heading into its nineties, it measures the dominant activities of the 1930s—agriculture and manufacturing— far more reliably than it gauges the gig economy, digital technologies, and unpaid work like parenting or caregiving.[9] There have been any number of national academies reports, academic conferences, and learned articles that propose substantive new measures and approaches, but progress is glacial.[10]

Employment data are similarly inflexible. The focus of much of official statistics has been on measuring unemployment—the "hole"—rather than employment—the "doughnut."[11] Yet it has become clearer that employment increasingly is braided across multiple employers and job spells rather than just one lifetime job, that earnings levels and growth matter as much as simply having a job, and that gender equality and income are very important. Yet the official employment measure has remained unchanged: internationally, "an employed person is someone in paid employment, including a family business, who, during the reference week, worked for at least one hour, or was temporarily absent due to personal reasons (e.g., illness, holiday, parental leave) or economic reasons (e.g., industrial action, reduction in economic activity, suspension of production).[12] And the data are collected in the same way they have been for decades—using surveys—despite alarming drops in response rates and concerns about the quality of those responses that are collected.[13]

A third reason agencies continue to produce these metrics is implicit in the earlier discussion. The apparatus of official statistics is designed to produce consistent measures of the same construct over time that are also internationally comparable. That mindset militates against rapid change, which is both a good thing and a bad thing. We do need a long view of how the economy is changing. But we need more up-to-date monitoring of what's changing, why, and how.

To understand why it's so hard to change a measurement once it is in place, we need to look more closely at how official statistics get started and how they evolve. The key factors are the importance of the problem a particular measure was intended to solve, the role of innovative people in developing a measurement approach, and the evolution of organizations to create the measure. GDP is probably the most studied measure, so we'll use that as the illustrative example.

HOW THE GDP CAME TO BE

In the mid-seventeenth century in Europe, states that couldn't pay for a powerful military were at risk of being taken over by states that could. So, the problem to be solved was a military one—kings needed to figure out how much people could be taxed to pay for the war.[14] As David Pilling says in his 2018 book, *The Growth Delusion*, "Rulers rule with rulers: they measure."[15] Measurement was necessary to determine who should be taxed and how much. A bad taxation strategy could drain the nation's resources so much that the government could be overthrown (which happened in France) or compromise future growth (which happened with the Spanish Empire). States that used more strategic forms of taxation could defeat richer countries.[16] England and Wales were able to figure out in 1655 how to finance the Second Anglo-Dutch War through the services of an English economist, William Petty, who estimated the assets, income, and expenditures of the population.[17] That enabled them to compete successfully against France, which didn't introduce sufficient economic measurements until 1781, when Louis XVI's finance minister, Jacques Necker, created a system of national accounts in his *Compte rendu au roi*, or "Report to the king."[18]

The approaches to modern-day national income measurement languished until the Great Depression and World War II forced change.[19] The United States only had sketchy information about the extremity, length, and causes of the economic crisis. The economic theory at the time said that the economy would return itself to full employment equilibrium, but the only data that were available were stock market indices, freight car loadings, and some measures of industrial production.[20] Without a single measure, policy makers were left pulling together disparate measurements and anecdotes that did not tell the whole story in a systematic and reliable way, even as the long lines of unemployed workers made it clear that something needed to be done. In 1927 when the economist John Maynard Keynes called the United Kingdom's statistical apparatus so "deplorably deficient" that it left policy makers and their advisers groping in "barbaric darkness,"[21] he could equally have been talking about the United States or the world at large.

The development of modern-day measures of economic activity to respond to the crisis was path-breaking. Indeed two of the academics who developed the intellectual foundations, Richard Stone in the United Kingdom and Simon Kuznets in the United States, both earned the Nobel Prize in economics.[22] The approach that they took was to carefully measure the component parts of national income and put them together into one measure that could act as a call for policy action.

How did this transformation in measurement happen in the 1930s? In three words: mission, people, and organization. In 1932, the US Senate was desperate to respond to the economic crisis, so it asked the Department of Commerce (DOC) to provide estimates of national income for 1929–1931. Nobody in the DOC knew how to construct national income accounts, so the DOC turned to a nonprofit academic institution—the National Bureau of Economic Research (NBER)—to provide people who could help.[23] The NBER's Simon Kuznets led the small team of researchers who worked at the NBER and the Bureau of Foreign and Domestic Commerce and generated those estimates by hand from the data within the Bureau. When the data showed that economic activity had been halved between 1929 and 1932, the link between data, theory, and action was immediate.[24]

First, the data showed that from 1929 to 1932, the economy had been in a low, and apparently stable, level of economic activity for three years, with no tendency to break out of that equilibrium by itself.[25] So there was a need for direct action by the government.

Second, by breaking out the overall economic activity levels into component parts by industry and use, the data supported a theoretical framework that enabled the government to see the likely result of various policy initiatives intended to stimulate the economy, and choose the ones that did in fact reduce unemployment.

Third, the data enabled policy makers to identify which sectors were hurting the most, and galvanized government action. Work relief programs and the New Deal were established: President Roosevelt used the new and better data to design and launch his Recovery Project.[26]

While the Great Depression was a major galvanizing force for the adoption of GDP, World War II was another. As a 2008 article in the *Journal of Economic Perspectives* titled "Taking the Pulse of the Economy: Measuring GDP" points out, the new NBER-generated estimates "helped in assessing the economy's overall productive capacity and the impact of moving from consumer spending on goods and services to federal government spending on tanks, materials, and other war expenditures."[27] In sum, the exigency of the war effort led the United States to publish the first gross national product (GNP) statistic in 1942. Two years later, when the allied powers met in Bretton Woods, New Hampshire, in 1944, and established the World Bank and the International Monetary Fund (IMF), they needed a common measure to identify projects for funding. The World Bank and the IMF adopted the methodologies from the United States and Great Britain and GNP became an international measure of economic activity.

The measurement of national income has, of course, evolved and become more sophisticated over time from the initial motivating question: given government war expenditures, how much would be left for civilians to consume?[28] GNP, which measures the output of a country's citizens, regardless of where they live, gave way in the 1990s to GDP, which measures the economic activity within a country, regardless of who owns the activity. Currently GDP is estimated using three conceptually identical approaches—one measures production, or value added, by each industry; the second measures income by source (compensation of employees, profits, interest, etc.); the third measures expenditures by consumers, businesses, government, and net exports. The three approaches generally produce roughly comparable results.[29] However, the intrinsic noise in generating the estimates is huge. The data for calculating GDP are generally collected from surveys or from administrative sources that generate data, such as tax records. Thousands upon thousands of data sources are combined by hundreds of statisticians to generate the single number that represents GDP;[30] and the work is done across multiple agencies.[31] For example, "nominal sales are collected by the Census Bureau, prices are collected by the Bureau of Labor Statistics (BLS), and real and nominal GDP are constructed by the Bureau of Economic Analysis (BEA) using these and other data sources."[32]

The consequences of the development of the GDP measure are difficult to overstate. GDP helped inform decisions about how to fund the Marshall Plan, which helped rebuild postwar Western Europe. It became part of US federal law; for example, the 1946 Employment Act set GDP targets for economic growth. Generations of policy makers used GDP measures to inform deficit-spending policies to stimulate economic activity. Some argue that it led to the United States being more active in foreign policy, since comparative GDP measures conclusively demonstrated its status as a world economic power. In other words, measurement does matter—in the broadest sense, the use of data rather than cronyism to allocate resources was at the heart of the spread of American democratic ideals.

A DIFFICULT TASK: THE PROBLEM WITH SINGLE MEASURES

Despite its widespread use, there have been ample warnings of the limitations of GDP measurement. Kuznets, the leader of the original national income project, repeatedly pointed out that income measures were not the same as welfare measures. He eventually broke with the Department of Commerce for its leaders' refusal to include unpaid work in income statistics.[33] As the former head of the National Bureau of Economic Research, Martin Feldstein wrote in an academic article in 2017, "in practice, national income concepts have been intentionally defined in ways that fall far short of measuring even economic well-being, let alone the broader well-being of individuals as influenced by matters like the environment and crime."[34]

There are many, many assumptions that were made in creating a single national statistic. As was well recognized at the time,[35] some of those assumptions were quite sweeping. For example, we have to compare the change in GDP over time so that we can see whether the economy has grown or shrunk. But, since GDP is based on spending, which is the price paid for goods and services times the quantity of those goods and services, a comparison of economic growth involves adjusting for prices (sometimes called "constant dollar" or "real" GDP). Price adjustments cause huge headaches. For example, sometimes an increase in the price of an item reflects an improvement in quality, and failing to take account of this would lead to an under-estimate of real GDP. A computer now may cost the same as a few years ago, but you get much more from it. How much more is that computer worth today than it was a few years ago? For that matter, how do you compare GDP that measured the value of goods and services forty years ago (where computers and cell phones didn't exist) with GDP now? As the MIT economists Erik Brynjolfsson and Adam Saunders point out, we know less about the economy now than we did twenty-five years ago, and are missing measuring trillions of dollars in benefits.[36]

And then there are other headaches that have been known for many years, as Robert F. Kennedy pointed out. How should we value household services, since a meal produced and eaten at home does not contribute to GDP, but the same meal produced and eaten at a restaurant does? Do financial services, which generate huge incomes, actually add value? How should we count environmental degradation, the measurement of intangible assets, and asset depreciation?

The rapidly changing economy in the new millennium poses many additional measurement challenges. How do we value new goods and services that save time—a precious but unmeasured asset? How do we value new products and services that have transformed economic activity, such as those provided by Facebook, Amazon, and Google, which do not have an explicit price associated with their use? As if the conceptual gaps weren't challenging enough, there also are systemic problems with the processes the statistical agencies follow to produce these numbers. GDP statistics are not only produced with a long time lag, they are also error-prone. The data components that make up GDP take a long time to collect, so the Bureau of Economic Analysis produces the first quarterly GDP estimate the month after the quarter ends, then a revision the following month, and then another revision following that month—so either the government reacts slowly or with insufficient information.

It's also well known that if the institutions calculating GDP are not sufficiently protected from political influences, the GDP framework can be easy to game. When I taught econometrics to classes that included statisticians from developing countries, several openly acknowledged that their job was to ensure that the measure of their countries' GDP per capita—a key measure for qualifying for World Bank loans—was on target.[37] In fact, the chief statistician of Greece was threatened with jail in 2013 for *refusing* to cook the books and is still being criminally prosecuted.[38] And while Diane Coyle lightheartedly points out in her excellent 2015 book *GDP: A Brief but Affectionate History* that European statisticians increased GDP by adding in estimates for prostitution and drugs, she is also making a very serious point about GDP's fragility as a useful metric.

Robert F. Kennedy said, in a different context, "Some men see things as they are, and ask why. I dream of things that never were, and ask why not?" So why have we not changed the best-known national statistics? Why can't we generate new measures that are more useful? It's not that the problems are unknown. Chapter 1 opened by citing former BLS Commissioner Janet Norwood, who was one of the most influential leaders of the federal system and produced a detailed indictment of the current system over twenty years ago.[39] Very good economists, such as Nobel Laureate Joseph Stiglitz; former director of NBER's Program on Technological Progress and Productivity Measurement Ernie Berndt; former Federal Reserve Board senior economist Carol Corrado; and Erik Brynjolffson have devoted a lot of time to suggesting improvements.[40] The Bureau of Economic Analysis's Brian Moyer calls GDP "the Ultimate Data Science Project."[41]

It's just extremely hard to effect change in the production of national statistics in general. To understand why, it's worth doing a deep dive into the process of generating the primary instrument that agencies use to collect data—surveys.

CHANGE IS DIFFICULT

The process of generating a statistical measure using survey data is a bit like running a factory. Understanding it requires looking at the inputs (data collection), the way the ingredients are put together (by government agency staff), and the machinery that is involved in government measurements of the economy (the organization). To see all the steps involved with running a survey, read the very helpful 100-page document put out by the White House's Office of Information and Regulatory Affairs Office, titled *Questions and Answers When Designing Surveys for Information Collections.*[42] I'll illustrate with the example of the Current Population Survey (CPS),[43] which is an important data source for many reasons, but is probably best known for measuring employment and unemployment in the US.

The first step is to determine the *need* for the measurement. The impetus for employment data, yet again, was the Great Depression.[44] Then *money* needs to be appropriated by Congress. In the case of employment data, there is a standing appropriation; getting new funding for new surveys can take several years, and the agency is often asked to run multiple pilot projects to test feasibility.

The next step is to *define the concept*. In the case of employment, it's whether or not a person has a job, which is defined as working at least one hour a week in the survey week.[45] This is also the international standard used in labor force surveys across the world. Of course, there are many other possibilities; we will discuss those later.[46]

Then the agency has to decide how to *administer* the survey—whether to use the internet (online), mail, phone, or in person. The costs are vastly different—based on my experience in the survey world, they can run roughly $1,800 per respondent for a sixty-minute, in-person interview, but about $200 by mail. The types of questions, the response rates, and the quality of the responses can vary dramatically, of course, depending on the survey mode. The CPS is largely an in-person interview because of the complexity of the questions, although some are conducted over the phone.

Once a measure is defined—usually with the time-consuming and laborious input of many experts and stakeholders, the next step is to *design a question* that can be answered in a way that gets as close as possible to the underlying truth—what psychometricians call "construct validity." This is really hard, and some scientists argue that it is not possible to do.[47] Indeed, it takes about nine pages of questions for a survey interviewer to probe the different facets of employment in the CPS.[48]

Then the survey undergoes an extensive internal agency review that can take many months if not years. Once that is finished, the survey must be cleared by the Office of Management and Budget (OMB) in the Executive Office of the President. Information about the proposed survey must be posted as a notice in the *Federal Register* (the publication of the US federal government that issues proposed and final administrative regulations of federal agencies) for sixty days to allow the public to comment on the proposed survey design and questions. Then the agency must review all of the comments. Once the comments are addressed in some fashion, agencies have to post a second notice describing to the public how they addressed the comments. The package is simultaneously transmitted to OMB, which then has a total of sixty days to review any new comments. At each step of the process, time must be allocated between when text is submitted to the *Federal Register* and when it is actually published.

Then the survey itself has to be designed. The *population* has to be defined. In the case of the CPS, it's the civilian non-institutional population—so it excludes the military and incarcerated individuals. It's clearly prohibitive in terms of time, burden, and cost to ask the question of everyone in the United States, so a *sample* has to be chosen. That sample is not a simple random sample—again for cost reasons, it has to be stratified. In the case of the CPS, of 2,000 geographic areas in the United States, only about eight hundred are chosen that represent "urban and rural areas, different types of industrial and farming areas, and the major geographic divisions of each state."[49] Then the *sample size* has to be determined to ensure that the survey has sufficient information to be statistically valid at the level needed—in the case of the CPS, the goal is to provide national data, and so 60,000 households are surveyed on a monthly basis. This sample is too small to provide statistically reliable monthly estimates at the local level—and even at the state level for the smaller US states simply because their populations are too small.

Then the task turns to collecting the data. In operational terms, the work requires the data equivalent of the workers on a car assembly line. A *field staff* must be hired. The CPS is conducted by the US Census Bureau, which owns the national Master Address File and has a trained field staff that is dedicated to the monthly CPS survey. *Training materials* need to be developed—in the case of the CPS, field interviewers are exposed to classroom lectures, discussion, practice, observation, home-study materials, and on-the-job training. A great deal of time and energy is spent on this aspect because interviewer error can substantially reduce the quality of a survey.

The nitty gritty of the work is unbelievable. For example, IT staff develop *interview software* that is specifically designed to capture the responses, and that must be bug-free (which is extremely difficult to do with complex responses). Failure can be expensive! The highest-profile example of failure was the 2010 Decennial Census, where a contract failure meant that the handheld devices provided to interviewers were too unreliable and had to be replaced by paper forms—the resultant cost was estimated at $2–3 billion.[50] Because it is so important to get response rates as high as possible, field managers develop *protocols* to ensure that the interviewers get responses without harassing respondents. In a less high-profile but very problematic case, a design failure led to a "hole" in the 1997 National Longitudinal Survey of Youth data. This expensive and important survey is extensively used to understand employment and education over the course of a life, beginning with cohorts of youth age twelve to sixteen.[51] A screening error in the survey design (potential respondents learned from their neighbors that if they answered "yes" to the question about whether there was an eligible youth in the house, they would be subjected to a long burdensome survey) meant that households with youths were more likely to refuse to be screened. The result was substantial damage to the representativeness of the survey for the very cohort it was designed to study.[52]

Then there is *post-survey* processing. Since only a representative sample of people is surveyed, each response needs to be weighted to provide an estimate of the responses from people who were not surveyed or who do not respond. This process of generating survey weights that reflect the response rates can take a great deal of time and expert judgment.[53] In addition, even if a respondent fills out a survey, some questions may be answered incorrectly or not at all. In the American Community Survey, for example, Mexican men of working age are most likely to incorrectly mark themselves as citizens. Survey analysts need to first understand when the data may be incorrect and then calculate values for such missing or incorrect items.[54] Despite the care and professionalism of survey teams, there are still many concerns about the level of error. As Bob Groves, a former director of the Census Bureau, and Lars Lyberg, senior advisor at Statistics Sweden have pointed out, because survey statisticians are not close enough to their user base, they don't fully understand how errors can creep in and therefore can't correct for them.

Of course, once the data have been collected and processed, they have to be made available for use by students and career counselors, by farmers, by local governments, and by small businesses. So the data have to be disseminated. This is tough, because statistical agencies are required by law to protect the confidentiality of respondents. There can be both civil and criminal penalties if they fail. Title 13 of the US Code, which protects data that are collected by the Census Bureau (like the CPS), has penalties of up to $250,000 or imprisonment for not more than five years, or both, for wrongful disclosure.

The challenge with disseminating data is that every time data are released, there is a risk of a respondent's confidential information being disclosed.[55] And there is deep distrust of the federal government collecting data. Not only has the American public's level of trust in government generally dropped from over 80 percent in the late 1950s to about 20 percent in 2016,[56] but also the decision by Secretary of Commerce Wilbur Ross to put a citizenship question on the 2020 Decennial Census was met with an explosion of more general concern about the motives for federal data collection.[57] This concern is not without foundation—historian Margo Anderson has documented the role of the Census Bureau in providing data that were used for the internment of Japanese Americans.[58]

The effects on measurement are nontrivial. In a recent Census Bureau study, nearly a quarter of respondents were "very concerned" or "extremely concerned" that their answers to the 2020 Census would be used against them; the rates were highest among non-Hispanic Asians, African Americans, Hispanics, and respondents who were not proficient in English.

Finally, and ironically, as mentioned in chapter 1, after all the effort taken to get the best data possible from a survey, the application of disclosure protection rules to mask individual responses substantially damages data quality.[59] And, as with any data, if you want to go and work with the original survey rather than the released data, it can take more than a year to get approval to do so in a secure environment in the federal statistical research data system.

INFLEXIBILITY IS BAKED IN

If you think this survey process is a long, time-consuming road, you are absolutely right. But it can be worse for the alternatives. One example is the use of administrative records for analysis. Nancy Potok, former chief statistician of the United States and former deputy director of the Census Bureau, has estimated the whole process from concept to implementation can take as long as ten years.[60] And if you wonder how these agencies incorporate the diverse and competing interests of the community, you're right to wonder. The agencies do their best, but community engagement is equally bureaucratic and slow—it's a big country and there are many voices to listen to.

You may have noticed that when new ideas and approaches were needed to calculate GDP, the genesis of those ideas came from the two academics mentioned earlier, Simon Kuznets and Richard Stone, as well as Colin Clark. The key staff came not from the statistical agencies, but from a nonprofit: the National Bureau of Economic Research. However, the academic community is now largely separate from most agencies rather than integral to the operational processes. Organizations like the NBER's Conference for Research on Income and Wealth (Kuznets had a hand in establishing it),[61] which is intended to provide new ideas to statistical agencies, and the Committee on National Statistics produce many such ideas, but it can take years for them to be adopted. For example, the Bureau of Labor Statistics has taken more than ten years to modernize consumer expenditures data collection.

Contrast this federal machinery with the private sector. Many of the most successful private companies of our time use data and statistics to figure out what people want (or, less ethically, decide for them), and then to build businesses around meeting those desires. Amazon does this with product recommendations. Google does it with search results. Facebook does it with feeds of posts and news stories. If businesses are not innovative, and don't constantly respond to their customers, they don't survive. This includes constantly changing processes and even discontinuing products or projects.

Of course, federal agencies have a different remit from the private sector, which is to establish the statistical standards for high-quality data that people can trust, and to protect that data. There is a great exchange in Allan Bennett's play *Forty Years On* between the protagonist Franklin and the school headmaster. Franklin asks, "Have you ever thought, Headmaster, that your standards might perhaps be a little out of date?," to which the headmaster responds, "Of course they're out of date. Standards always are out of date. That is what makes them standards."[62] The problem is knowing how to strike the balance between ossification and quality protection. As Ronald Reagan famously said, "No government ever voluntarily reduces itself in size. Government programs, once launched, never disappear. Actually, a government bureau is the nearest thing to eternal life we'll ever see on this earth!"

Although I've unpacked the most well-known issues with the statistical machinery by highlighting those concerning the measurement of employment and income, the issues are there because these are hard problems. Attempts to circumvent the federal statistical system are costly and tend to fail. Look at the way that the US government itself tried to generate data about jobs after the Great Recession hit in 2008. The American Recovery and Reinvestment Act was passed to create a massive fiscal stimulus, but rather than turning to the federal statistical system to generate information about the resultant economic activity, funding recipients were instructed to generate their own estimates of jobs created and retained. The results were required to be reported on Recovery.gov, an entirely new online system. Alas, the reporting mechanism failed the test of reliability: Despite the fact that thousands of companies spent millions of hours painstakingly putting the information together, the data have not been a reliable source of information. Indeed, since mid-2016, the Recovery.gov site has shown a "404" error, indicating that the site no longer exists and providing no reason or further details. There are few digital remnants of the herculean efforts of awardees to manually report the results,[63] at least partly because they were not categorized as official statistical data requiring ongoing access.

So, to return to Robert F. Kennedy's question, this chapter has described why measurement is hard and why our core measures are lacking. Measurement is getting even harder, because of changes in the economy and society, increasing demands for data, and the increasing inadequacy of surveys.

Chapter 3 describes in detail why statistical agencies are not structured to respond to change. They are not designed to be dynamic and innovative. They are given congressional funding to produce consistent, trusted data via a set of measures that often were determined a long time ago. While the staff work hard to collect and process data using the tools and approaches that they've been trained to use and to apply the standards that are important to maintain, there is no impetus for change, and new measures will not emerge by themselves.

It may be that the 2020 coronavirus outbreak has provided the catalyst for some change. At a time when decision makers desperately needed high-quality information about what was happening to jobs at the local level, the old measures were insufficient. Unemployment data from the Current Population Survey had to be collected by phone, rather than in person, and the way that estimates were generated for the forty smallest states and regions resulted in unknown changes in the quality of unemployment estimates.

Any change has to break down the persistence of the institutional processes—the factory production line itself—and the way they are structured.[64] I describe that structure in chapter 3.

3 SET UP TO FAIL

The organizational failings have not gone unnoticed.

Each year the White House Office of Management and Budget produces reports related to the production of federal statistics. The cover letter to OMB's fiscal 2018 "Statistical Programs of the United States Government" notes that "federal statistical agencies are striving to supplement or replace surveys that are more burdensome, counter falling levels of cooperation from the public on survey response, increase accuracy and relevance, and save money." The letter goes on, stating that OMB "looks forward to working closely with the Congress to build a 21st Century system of statistical measurement . . ." Contained in this closing is the subtle acknowledgement that the changes needed are fundamental in nature.

The same drum was beaten as long ago as 1995, when President Clinton's budget included this statement: "Our measurements of economic performance are perforated with gaps in areas of vital importance, areas of public policy concern are poorly measured if measured at all, the data gathering system imposes too great a workload on both the agencies that gather the data and the firms that provide it, and the resulting product goes underutilized in a world in which timely and accurate information is often the key to competitive business success."[1]

There can be serious consequences if the statistical organization fails. One of the best examples of the importance of high-quality statistics is the Greek economy. As many tell it, the Greek statistical agency falsified reports between 1997 and 2009, which contributed to Greece's bankruptcy,[2] but benefited incumbent politicians to the extent that when Andreas Georgiou became chief statistician in 2010 and refused to continue the practice, he was threatened with prosecution and jail time. The international concern with preserving good data practices was such that the American Statistical Association Board sent a letter signed by nine Nobel Laureates, forty-six organizations, and more than 1,100 other individuals to Greek officials that stated, "The continued prosecution of Georgiou undermines the current production of Greek statistical figures, the accuracy and objectiveness of which are paramount for attracting foreign investment and ending Greece's cycles of economic crises."[3]

The US statistical system is far from corrupt, but executive branch memos, such as those detailing the need for reorganizing the Census Bureau, the Bureau of Labor Statistics, and the Bureau of Economic Analysis into a single agency,[4] make it clear that there are foundational problems that go beyond simply changing policy or providing budget guidance. The system is fragmented, and the consequences are serious.

THE CONSEQUENCES

Simply put, the consequences of the current system fragmentation are duplication and inconsistency as well as inefficiency at all levels, with limited accountability to stakeholders. Norwood argued that these flaws had led to a clear decline in the supremacy of the US system starting in the 1940s; since then, the decline has only accelerated.

Duplication is a serious issue for data quality. Each agency has a different mandated mission, and some must use only their own data for that mission because other agencies collecting similar data are prohibited from sharing them. In fact, there can be draconian consequences if agencies don't follow the rules. For example, Section 6103 of Title 26 of the US Code authorizes both civil and criminal penalties for unlawful disclosures of tax data.[5] The result—as Norwood pointed out over twenty years ago—is that the same basic data are developed in many places, with different concepts, time periods, and classification structures.[6]

For example, while most countries have one definitive list of businesses called the Business Register that is used for surveys and censuses, as well as the production of the National Income and Product Accounts, the United States has two. The Bureau of Labor Statistics has a business register of employers derived from state-level reports that is used to produce information about business employment and earnings at the county level, as well as other statistics. The US Census Bureau has a different business register derived from Internal Revenue Service data that is used to produce information about business activity, such as total sales and also payroll and employment. The Bureau of Labor Statistics is not authorized by law to use the same tax data that the Census Bureau can access. The result is that the same business might be classified in different industries and show substantive differences on measures of industry productivity growth.[7] Payroll differences at the state level between the two agencies "could have a significant impact on the allocation of state Medicaid funds, which uses Bureau of Economic Analysis per capita state personal income to determine the federal share of payments for each state."[8] This also creates a lot of work for Bureau of Economic Analysis analysts who have to reconcile the data received from the Bureau of Labor Statistics with that received from the Census Bureau to calculate their combined statistical measures.

Inconsistency and inefficiency are rampant as well. An instructive example is the data used to produce information on how much people are spending—a critical indicator of economic activity. Data on nominal spending are collected by the Census Bureau using surveys with declining response rates and irregular responses at different periods of time. Those numbers need to be adjusted for inflation; data on prices are collected by the Bureau of Labor Statistics using a different sample and different levels of aggregation. They "don't even match at the retail outlet level, let alone the item level."[9] Suggestions for using different data sources, such as supermarket scanner data rather than multisource, multimode surveys, were made twenty years ago. However, while "researchers have made progress . . . U.S. statistical agencies have not yet implemented the vision of using such data for dramatic improvements in measurement for official statistics."[10]

Another example of inefficiency is the production of statistics that enable researchers and policy makers to trace the connection between education and job outcomes. Limited education measures are captured by the National Center for Education Statistics, and placement and earnings outcomes are available only at the Statistics of Income division of the Internal Revenue Service or the US Census Bureau.[11] And, while the federal agencies have been collaborating to produce a college scoreboard,[12] the measures suffer from similar problems—for example, students are only included if they applied for federal student aid, and measures can be biased because they don't correct for the quality of students in each institution. The national data also don't capture the full complexity of the education process because state and local agencies hold many of the key data elements.[13] This means that even if they could access the data, someone doing research on education and job outcomes would need to coordinate data from multiple agencies.

Finally, while most agencies work hard to be accountable, this is not always the case, as is troublingly evident in a recent high-profile attempt to change the way in which confidentiality is protected at the US Census Bureau. While protecting confidentiality is essential to the operation of a statistical agency, and there is no question that there is a need to update the approach, the agency upset large numbers of its constituency by instituting new policies to protect confidentiality without fully consulting with the user community. There are thousands of governments, businesses, nonprofits, and academics who have invested billions of dollars and volumes of research in systems and tools that use Census data for doing their work;[14] they were not consulted. One highly influential scientist has argued that the approach "will severely damage data infrastructure indispensable for basic research and policy analysis."[15] The failure to include users in the decisions have led more than four thousand scholars, planners, and journalists to sign a petition demanding input.[16]

So what is the solution? The answer is not more money, although agency advocates often argue that lack of resources stymies development.[17] But more money to do more of the same thing is not going to solve the problem. A former high-level administrator in the Bureau of Labor Statistics often told me that the draconian cuts that Ronald Reagan made in the early 1980s were the best thing that could have happened to public data collection—because the cuts forced statistical agencies to rethink the way in which they did business. The same is true thirty years later. More money to perpetuate the inefficiencies that are endemic in the current system without rethinking and introducing different ways of generating leadership and innovation in the production of data will not succeed in creating new trusted public measures.[18] But in order to recommend change, it's necessary to begin by understanding how the statistical system operates.

STATISTICAL AGENCIES IN GENERAL

If you peruse the websites of statistical agencies in the United States as well as most developed countries, you see that they have the same mandate—to produce independent statistics that inform decision-making. And if you look at the annual meetings of the Chief Statisticians (both the United Nations Conference of European Statisticians and U.N. Statistical Commission), they are all facing the same problems.[19]

A key problem is how to make use of new data to produce unbiased statistics while protecting privacy and confidentiality. US statistical agencies recognize that the old—often survey-based—ways of collecting data are no longer the dominant source of information outside of the world of official statistics, and that survey response rates and quality can be expected to continue to decline despite the institution of costly countermeasures. They also recognize that the amount of data available through other mechanisms is continually increasing—the technology company IDC estimates that the data generated by the economy will reach 180 zettabytes by 2025.[20] The agencies recognize that managing that scale of information is impossible with the current fragmented organization of federal statistics agencies. The technological capacity to manage this data is not there—particularly in the United States. A recent opinion piece in the *Washington Post* referred to government technology as "the design equivalent of installing a hand-cranked engine on a Tesla or communicating with Alexa via smoke signal."[21] The human capacity in government to manage this data is not there either. Federal salaries and conditions can't compete with Amazon and other for-profit data companies, particularly in a world of unpredictable government shutdowns, hiring freezes, and funding cuts. And, even though the United States has world-class statisticians, economists, and data scientists, many are choosing to work in academia and the private sector. Partnerships between government agencies can be challenging to execute effectively due to the complex mechanisms in place for contracting, joint ventures, and other collaboration vehicles. Although there are several examples of federal-state intergovernmental partnerships on paper, there are often complaints on the state end that such relationships resemble more a federal dictatorship than an equal sharing of interests and knowledge.

But the two biggest problems are that there is no structural way to introduce new ideas into the warp and weave of the current system, and there is no budgetary incentive to do so.

STRUCTURE OF US STATISTICAL AGENCIES

The way in which bureaucracies have evolved is a whole field of study,[22] and American federal bureaucracy is fascinating in its own right.[23] The two most important factors in understanding the current state of affairs with regard to the US statistical system are the organization—made up of multiple agencies—and how funds are allocated from both the executive and legislative branches of government.

Organization

Most countries have a single statistical agency (like Statistics New Zealand, Statistics Sweden, or Statistics Netherlands). The United States has no single agency—it has thirteen major statistical agencies and almost a hundred others; it is one of the most fragmented systems of any modern nation.[24] Individual statistical units were created when demand for information arose in a particular area (such as agriculture, health, and transportation). As a result, there are two statistical agencies in the US Department of Agriculture, two in the Department of Commerce, and one each in the Departments of Education, Justice, Transportation, Labor, Energy, Health and Human Services, and the Treasury. There are two statistical agencies for independent agencies— one at the National Science Foundation and one at the Social Security Administration.[25] Some cabinet agencies, such as the Department of Homeland Security and the Environmental Protection Agency, conduct statistical activities but do not house an officially recognized independent statistical agency or unit.

The decentralized US structure emerged for a commendable reason: to generate statistics that are more relevant because there is direct engagement with the communities providing and using the data. That approach to statistics would appear to be a good thing, but that has not been the case.

Janet Norwood, whom I've referenced in both chapters 1 and 2, identified the major structural issues in her 1995 book *Organizing to Count, Change in the Federal Statistical System.*[26] In it, Norwood described a federal statistical system that was not just disjointed, but also was doomed to fragment further without significant reform.[27] She was worried about a system with eleven principal statistical agencies and over seventy other significant statistical programs[28]—now there are many more. While each individual statistical agency or unit may be more or less responsive to parts of their larger agencies, the overall structure is paralyzed.

Coordination of the multiple agencies is left to the management and budgetary policy arm of government—the Office of Management and Budget within the Executive Office of the President. The extent of the OMB's reach matured over time as a result of the 1942 Federal Reports act, the 1980 Paperwork Reduction Act (PRA) and its 1995 amendment, the 2001 Information Quality Act, and the 2018 Foundations for Evidence Based Policymaking Act.[29] Statistical policy and standards are developed within a small branch of the Office of Information and Regulatory Affairs (OIRA) at OMB. That branch office, called Statistical and Science Policy (SSP), is headed by the chief statistician of the United States, a statutory position created by the PRA to coordinate the decentralized federal statistical system. This position was a successor to a previous position in OMB, the assistant director for statistical policy, which at one time consisted of an office of 150 people but was organized out of existence during the Carter administration in an effort to cut White House costs.[30] The OMB currently holds extensive oversight authority and has mandates across the statistical agencies that include setting standards for data classifications such as industry, product, and occupational codes, metropolitan statistical areas, and race and ethnicity categories; privacy and confidentiality protection; data quality; operations efficiency; scientific integrity; budget; safeguarding the independence and objectivity of federal statistics; designation of official statistical agencies and units under the Confidential Information Protection and Statistical Efficiency Act (title 3 of Pub.L. 115-435);[31] regulation of how agencies classify the sensitivity of data and provide access to data users; methods and best practices for data collection and dissemination; data collection approval (when data are collected from ten or more respondents); authorization to promulgate regulations and orders; long-range planning; and evaluation of program performance.[32] The Interagency Council on Statistical Policy (ICSP), chaired by the chief statistician, regularly brings together statistical officials from twenty-four agencies to advise OMB, strategically plan the future of federal statistics, collaborate on cross-agency priorities, and direct the research agenda of the Federal Committee on Statistical Methodology. The ICSP serves as a common source from which each agency can receive advice on standards and policy.[33] The SSP branch of OIRA has substantial scope—its oversight role spans the more than one hundred agencies that have direct funding for statistical activities (which include survey design, data collection and analysis, forecasting, and modeling) of $500,000 or more.[34] However, because SSP is only a branch of the OIRA with fewer than ten staff members and little visibility within OMB, it cannot effectively manage the sprawling statistical system. The office has no direct budgetary authority over the agencies, and so its role is more one of coordination, production of guidelines, and dissemination of information and working papers. The current situation embodies the worst of all possible worlds: fragmented operational management and funding with inadequately resourced central direction and oversight, resulting in a Frankenstein's monster of decentralized and centralized elements.

Study after study has pointed to the inadequacy of resources dedicated to coordinating the statistical system. A commission appointed by President Carter to study the issue recommended that a coordination office in the Executive Office of the President (what became OMB) should have a staff of 200. The commission's lead called the lack of "effective capacity for central coordination . . . a crippling loss."[35] The Congressional Research Service, in 1992, compared coordination of the statistical system to "an opera without a conductor."[36] The Government Accountability Office (GAO) pointed out in 1995 that "a staff of five is not sufficient to do the detailed budget reviews necessary to ensure the coordination of federal statistical policy" in addition to SSP's other duties.[37] Despite these repeated critiques, SSP is overshadowed in OIRA by four branches reviewing federal regulations, and the chief statistician's staff still numbers just eight today plus three to five rotating detailees from other agencies—a far cry from the dozens of staffers responsible for operating statistical institutes in other smaller countries with much less complex systems.

As a result, while OMB has general oversight of each statistical agency, the agencies themselves are responsible for day-to-day operations and the timely and accurate distribution of expected statistics, resulting in the duplication and inefficiencies discussed in the sections that follow.

Budget

The embedding of statistical agencies within separate departments across the federal government is a huge challenge. It means that each agency head has to make the case for resources not only through multiple bureaucratic layers of their host department, but also to different authorization and appropriations committees. Since, almost by definition, departments will differentially value the contribution of statistics to their operational mission, this fragmentation induces great heterogeneity in what each statistical agency can produce.

This organizational arrangement leads to certain behaviors exhibited by those departments' leaders. As Norwood puts it, "Each new statistical agency that is created is placed in its own subject matter department where the Cabinet Officer in charge generally has neither the interest nor the knowledge to make trade-offs among the data programs in his own agency and those elsewhere in the government." The result is that the National Agricultural Statistics Service and the Economic Research Service must compete for funding against other USDA programs, like the Forest Service or the Grain Inspection Administration, rather than justifying their value relative to other government statistical expenditures.

One additional feature of the US system is that since the legislative branch, particularly the appropriations committees, control the agency budgets, agencies build long-term relationships with congressional representatives (and their staffers) to ensure funding continuity. These relationships can be more important than the relationships with the agency political appointees, such as Cabinet secretaries put in place by the White House. Career bureaucrats often refer to themselves as "weebies" when talking about changes in the White House (we be there before they came, and we be there after they leave); since changes in congressional representatives are much less frequent, the building of long-term capital with those representatives is important. The result for the various statistical agencies is that funding is not determined by one congressional committee that is focused on data; rather, in each committee, there are myriad competing interests for funding.[38]

The fragmented nature of the system also means that different congressional committees control funding decisions for each of the agencies. As a result, there are different congressional mandates as well as duplication of effort. And, because each agency is tightly tied to its constituency, interest groups develop around each measure—at the federal level (with programmatic agencies) and at the state and local level. With any change, a war of words begins between the various interest groups impacted by the change. As Clea Benson of *Congressional Quarterly Weekly* puts it: "data isn't an issue that has a naturally large and vocal constituency."[39] She goes further and refers to Andrew Reamer. "There are three groups that don't talk to each other very well: the people who use the data, the people who produce the data and the people who fund the data," Reamer said. "There are very few members of Congress who fully understand what these agencies do and why they are important."

The political dynamic for the Census Bureau is particularly difficult and the consequences are painfully obvious. The Decennial Census is much more important in the United States than in other countries. It is constitutionally authorized, used to draw congressional boundaries, and determines the allocation of about $6 trillion in federal funds. Its significance is hard to overstate. It is expected to cost over $15.5 billion in 2020, or a cost of $48 per man, woman, and child. It is the largest peacetime activity in the United States, and employs over half a million temporary census takers. Data collection has been very difficult to modernize—in addition to its complexity, Congress inadequately funds critical modernization research early in the decade, preferring to throw money at the Census later in the decade when it is too late to adequately develop, test, and put in place many significant design changes. Another contributor to the challenges of running the Census Bureau is the politics of the intense congressional oversight. The best example of the issues is the discussion about using statistical sampling to enumerate the population. Many eminent statisticians have argued that the current approach of physically counting every individual is error-prone; those errors systematically undercount racial minorities and low-income individuals, both because those individuals tend to be suspicious of government motives and, in the latter case, because they change addresses more often so they are hard to count.[40] The Census Bureau proposed a new methodology in 2000 that would have allowed sampling of the last 10 percent of households in each census tract if they hadn't responded to the census, in order to save time and money and focus on the harder-to-count population.[41] It also proposed to eliminate the undercounting of certain segments of the population by statistically adjusting the results to account for households that were missed. The House of Representatives sued the Commerce Department over using sampling for the nonresponders, resulting in a Supreme Court decision that sampling was unconstitutional for enumerating the population used to apportion congressional seats among the states. While statistically adjusting the census numbers to increase accuracy of population totals used for redistricting of congressional districts was constitutional, in the end, the technical experts at the bureau determined that the proposed adjustment would not make the census more accurate, and the bureau did not adjust the population count in 2000. Two decades later, the Census Bureau is planning to use administrative records to count approximately 8 million households that are not expected to respond to the 2020 Census. While this has not been politically controversial, a White House Executive Order instructing the Census Bureau to also create a file from administrative records differentiating citizens from noncitizens has generated tremendous political opposition. Although several countries, particularly in Europe, conduct their population censuses primarily using administrative records rather than a survey questionnaire, it is not at all clear whether the political climate in the US would permit that approach for the 2030 Census, even though it would increase accuracy and save billions of dollars.

There are two rather imprecise instruments that are generally intended to produce accountability in government. The first is reviews by the Government Accountability Office, the independent nonpartisan agency in the legislative branch of government established to audit executive branch programs and performance and report findings and recommendations back to Congress. The second is advisory committees, which are set up by agencies and used at many levels ranging from developing high-level strategic initiatives, to getting input from research communities, and even more broadly to identifying program priorities and program evaluation instruments, all the way down to the provision of input on very narrowly defined decisions, such as the peer review of individual research proposals.[42] The GAO audits and reviews are useful but infrequent and are conducted only for the largest federal programs. Advisory committees are numerous, and oversight staff (OMB and congressional staffers) are often the primary audience, customer, and enforcer of advisory committee reports.[43] However, those reports are often used to postpone decisions—there have been dozens of reports, for example, about how to use administrative records in surveys but very little action as a result of them. The reports of academic advisory committees—such as the National Academies of Sciences, Engineering, and Medicine—can be used to effect change but can also act as a bureaucratic way to delay change. In contrast to other countries, such as Germany, where the Wissenschaftsrat—the equivalent of US National Academies—is directly funded by the federal government, the National Academies derives its funds largely from commissioned reports from the agencies themselves. Possibly in response to different financial incentives, the Wissenschaftsrat produces fewer reports and recommendations, but much more attention is paid to them.[44] In the United States, advisory committees are often used to manage agency reputation, avoid "embarrassing situations," compensate for deficiencies in agency knowledge, and redress agency weakness that derives from instability or tumult inside the agency.[45]

Indeed, few reports that have been commissioned have resulted in a fundamental change in how the government collects and makes use of data, a notable exception being the recommendations of the Commission on Evidence-Based Policymaking, half of which were enacted into law a little more than a year after they were issued. In other words, it's difficult to create an entire new system to replace and improve upon the existing infrastructure.

In the private sector, inefficient operations would result in the demise of underperforming firms. There is no such discipline in the public sector. It is unrealistic to expect the staff in government agencies to unilaterally make fundamental changes to the way in which they do business. They are largely hired to do the tasks for which funds are appropriated, and as long as Congress provides funds to federal agencies to continue producing statistics using the same methodology, without funding or direction to undertake fundamental changes, there is limited budgetary incentive or flexibility to change.

POSSIBLE CHANGE AGENTS

Change is most likely to come from outside, primarily from the academic community: recall the critical role of Kuznets, Hicks, and Stone in developing GDP. There is no shortage of institutions providing advice, much of it grounded in deep data experience.

One set of institutions is tied to the academic community. The United States is in the fortunate position of having some of the world's greatest statisticians, economists, and data scientists in its universities, at least as measured by Nobel Prizes, publications, and citations. Many of these experts are interested in informing change in federal statistics. The National Bureau of Economic Research's Conference for Research on Income and Wealth (CRIW) brings together academic and government economists at regular meetings and produces books intended to improve key measurements of the federal system. The Committee on National Statistics at the National Academies is a standing committee of expert statisticians and economists that advises federal agencies on how to improve measurement and operations. The Council of Professional Associations on Federal Statistics convenes meetings of representatives of professional associations that interact with the federal statistical agencies that could draw on their expertise. Taken together, these institutions provide possible foundations that could, in principle, guide strategy. Unfortunately, even many of the great ideas that have come out of organizations like the CRIW about improving GDP measures have taken many years to implement,[46] and all too often the reports emanating from the National Academies are not acted upon.[47]

There has also been an attempt to get concrete suggestions from researchers through the Federal Statistical Research Data Centers, a network of twenty-nine physical centers that have been installed in universities and federal entities, with hundreds of researchers working on analytical projects.[48] Some of this access was a response to the concern identified by leading economists David Card, Raj Chetty, Martin Feldstein, and Emmanuel Saez who noted:

> The availability of detailed administrative data abroad has led to a shift in the cutting edge of empirical research in many important areas of social science away from the United States and toward the countries with better data access. Because the US retains worldwide leadership in the quality of its academic researchers, US-based researchers are often involved in research using administrative data from other countries.[49]

Unfortunately, the contribution of researchers to effecting change has been limited for various reasons. For one, since researchers' incentives are to publish, not help build data infrastructures, there are very few researchers who are willing to take the time to improve federal operations.[50] But it is important for them to do so. Take, for example, the 2016 experience of three top economists, David Evans, Richard Schmalensee, and Scott Murray. They discovered significant undercounts of online retail sales in the United States—an important component of GDP—and found that "the Census Bureau does not follow the methodology that it reports publicly—or at least a reasonable interpretation of what it reports— . . . it was so hard for even careful researchers to learn how Census actually collects and compiles its data and thus to discover whether or not the published data are accurate."[51] Indeed, during the coronavirus pandemic, just when the need for understanding the impact was greatest, the twenty-nine physical centers were forced to shut down and access to federal statistical data was no longer possible through the network.

In addition, while there is a deep bench of experts from which to draw for new ideas,[52] the organizational barriers are often too great for statistical agencies to implement the advice of the community to transform operations.

OPPORTUNITY FOR CHANGE

The structural flaws are deep, but that does not mean that the system should be dismantled. Three key characteristics of the current federal system are critical and must be retained: the trust in the quality of statistics produced by federal statistical agencies, the agencies' professionalism and independence from outside interference, and the ability to generate consistent measures over time. In common with other statistical agencies, the system of public data must serve as a "credible source of relevant, accurate, and timely statistics in one or more subject areas that are available to the public and policy makers."[53]

The trust in federal data providers to protect data is well placed. The culture of confidentiality in federal statistical agencies, combined with the statutory civil and felony penalties, is deeply ingrained in their operational structure. Their professionalism and independence is critical because, unlike the private sector, the agencies are in the business of providing data as a public good, not profiting from withholding them. The agencies are given protections through laws and OMB directives to help them remain independent and unswayed by external influences. Finally, they have a treasure trove of national-level data that can be used as benchmarks for consistency across time and space, as well as extensive staff experience in doing so.

The key to designing a new data system, then, is to determine how to maintain these features while coming up with new mechanisms for collecting and working with data in response to increasing demand for timely and granular information. Certainly, as argued in chapter 2, there is an enormous new opportunity to do so. The final report of the Commission on Evidence-Based Policymaking,[54] which focused on the insufficiency of current evidence to improve the operation of government programs, suggested building a new set of federal institutions to meet the need. The resulting Foundations for Evidence-Based Policymaking Act of 2018[55] established the positions of CDOs and chief evaluation officers and the mandate to improve statistical functions across agencies. The act also establishes an advisory committee to examine the options for establishing a National Secure Data Service. And the Federal Data Strategy has established a set of principles and practices for effecting change at the federal level.

The challenge is taking up the recommendations, building on existing strengths, and ensuring that they can influence the operations of statistical agencies. As discussed in this chapter, the current system is not geared for action. While we are seeing renewed interest in creating the structures necessary for better data collection and dissemination, creating new roles is not enough if those new roles are not part of a new structure that removes some of the organizational hurdles to implementing real change. The next chapter describes what lessons might be learned from the structure of other organizations that have filled the innovation gap.

4 A SUCCESSFUL MODEL

Building new public sector approaches to deal with new questions and new types of data might seem an overwhelming task. This chapter shows that new approaches are possible. One successful model is the Institute for Research on Innovation and Science (IRIS) at the University of Michigan, which was established in 2015. In four short years, IRIS started from scratch and built an infrastructure called UMETRICS (an acronym for Universities: Measuring the EffecTs of Research on Innovation, Competitiveness, and Science) that reimagines the way in which data are collected, privacy is protected, and new products are produced in response to new demands.[1]

The challenge IRIS faced in creating reliable measures from new sources of data was really hard with many risks. The risks of failure are legion: for example, in 2014 a (different) team of researchers at the University of Michigan thought they had figured out how to use a new source of social media data—looking at tweets for phrases like "I lost my job" to create new measures of job loss and job search.[2] Unfortunately, they ran into problems; five years later there is a somewhat rueful note on their website: "We are currently in the process of revisiting our original model, which began to deviate in its estimates around mid-2014. We will be updating this site soon with our new model, along with details on our new model."[3] There are many other examples of the risks of using the new types of data—cell phone, Facebook, retail trade, or sensor data to name just a few—to construct new indicators. A particularly well-known example of failure was an attempt to use Google searches to create better (real-time) indicators of the incidence of flu than the Centers for Disease Control and Prevention (CDC).[4] More real-time estimates of flu incidence could help doctors and hospitals better prepare for how many people are likely to come in and need flu-related services. Google tracked how many people searched for "flu" to estimate the incidence of flu in the United States for a number of flu seasons[5] and the approach worked really well in the 2009 to 2011 flu seasons, but it was very far off for the next years—predicting more than twice the number of doctor visits than actually occurred.[6]

Neither of these two examples, nor the struggles of the federal system, mean that we should give up on ever getting good data and good measurement again! There are many successful examples in the private sector, such as baseball's "Moneyball," where the Oakland A's famously used data to build a better baseball team,[7] and Harrah's Casinos, which used data to compete and innovate.[8] One lesson of IRIS is that it takes a long time to get measurements right, and they can't be developed in the abstract. The measures that IRIS created were developed because there was a demand to understand the underlying processes and there was a long-term commitment to get things right. That's how the GDP and unemployment measures were developed and why, for all their faults, they still have value.

Another lesson of IRIS is that many institutions can be found in the nonprofit sector and in almost every university or research think tank that have developed deep expertise and deep data knowledge in studying many fields—like education, housing, criminal justice, workforce, or transportation policy. Like the University of Michigan team, they have asked new questions, brought in new datasets, kicked the tires to find out if they were useful, admitted when they are wrong, and kept trying to improve economic and social measurement.

This chapter looks more deeply into the approach used by IRIS to design a new measurement system because it lays the groundwork for chapter 7's recommendations.

HOW IRIS CAME TO BE

IRIS was established by a group of universities and academics outside the federal system to answer a very specific question— what is the impact of research funding on scientific and economic activity? In some ways figuring out how to answer this question is just as important as figuring out how to measure GDP—economic activity—because it helps us figure out how to generate growth in the economy without more physical inputs, as the Nobel Prize–winning economist Paul Romer showed. He argued that new ideas are largely driven by investment in university research and people with problem-solving skills, and that we could do much better in figuring out how to invest in them.[9] Unfortunately, it's so hard to measure impact that most science agencies simply count publications and patents.

The challenge that IRIS faced was hard because measuring the impact of science is hard. In order to measure the links between research investments and the general performance of the economy, it's important to address three initial measurement challenges: *what* is funded, *who* is funded, and the *results*. That's hard enough, but the next measurement step—connecting each of those pieces—is even harder[10] because the connection is the transmission of ideas through networks of people in long, circuitous, and often nonlinear fashion, over quite long time periods. While it's true that the best way to transmit knowledge, as the director of the Manhattan Project, Robert Oppenheimer, famously said, is to wrap it up in a person,[11] it's hard to track people and their networks. Developing a system that traces through the effect of research funding on people, and networks of people, required building a whole new infrastructure—because survey approaches can't create those measures, and can't capture the links between them.[12]

In order to create the data and links necessary for analysis, IRIS built partnerships with both universities and federal agencies. One partner was the US Census Bureau so that data on individuals could be securely and confidentially linked to their employment and earnings from W-2s and unemployment insurance wage records as well as the businesses they start up.[13] Another partner was the National Center of Science and Engineering Statistics, which has survey data about the characteristics and plans of the recipients of doctoral degrees.[14]

The results have been amazing. Over thirty-five major universities have joined the Institute, with another thirty universities in various stages of agreement. The 2019 UMETRICS research data release includes transaction-level information on more than 392,000 sponsored project grants covering over $80 billion in R&D expenditures, including payments to more than

643,000 faculty, staff, students, and postdocs, more than $48 billion in vendor purchases, and nearly $13 billion in subcontracts to other research performers. Linkages to thousands of dissertations, eight million US patents, tens of millions of scientific publications, as well as public information on hundreds of thousands federal grants are included. In sum, UMETRICS brings together data from nearly fifty different sources and represents one of the first sustainable "big data" social science research infrastructures. Even better, a growing community of more than 120 researchers from around the world has made use of three annual UMETRICS data releases.

IRIS and institutions like IRIS show the way forward. The next chapters will further examine why and how new approaches have been successful, but for now, we'll start small and describe how the infrastructure was set up, how the measurement process worked (with repeated references to the experience of measuring GDP almost a century ago), and the new systems that were developed. We start with describing the measurement problem, and then how the solution appeared.

THE MEASUREMENT CHALLENGE

The challenge that faced IRIS at the beginning was fundamental. You would think that given the billions of dollars spent on science, we would know whether such expenditures are "worth it," but no—we don't know how much a nation should spend on science, what kind of science should be supported, or how much should be paid by the private or the public sector.[15] The estimates of the return on investment like the one for the Human Genome Project that estimated the return was $141 for every \$1 that was invested[16] sometimes stretch credulity (by way of comparison, the average return to the stock market is about \$.1 for every \$1 that is invested).

A new way of measuring was clearly called for—and in direct parallel to how the government asked economists for help with measuring GDP, Jack Marburger, the science advisor to President Bush, specifically challenged social scientists to answer questions like "How much should a nation spend on science? What kind of science? How much from private versus public sectors?" Responding to this call was a tall order, because it involves using all the social science and computer science tools available to researchers. While it is true that there was a pathway to doing so, it required creating a whole new approach to collecting and combining data. That's what IRIS did, led by its executive director, a research sociologist named Jason Owen-Smith, and his collaborators.

Let's unpack each one of the three measurement challenges—figuring out what is funded, who is funded, and the results.

Measurement Challenge 1: What Is Funded

There is quite limited information on *what* research is funded by the federal government. The agency in charge of capturing this information is the National Center for Science and Engineering Statistics (NCSES). Two of their surveys provide data on research and development (R&D) spending in the United States, but these surveys are limited in what they cover and their data are often used to try to answer questions beyond what the data can reasonably support.

One survey, the Survey of Federal Funds for Research and Development (often called simply the *Federal Funds Survey*), asks federal agencies to report their spending in different fields of research. However, the categories used in the surveys do not always line up with the categories used by the agencies in their own internal reporting. The data suffer when agencies are forced to slot their research into ill-fitting categories, as decisions about how to categorize research are made idiosyncratically by staff members who may make different judgment calls than their counterparts at another agency. In some cases, the categories are so broad as to lose meaning. For example, huge agencies like the Centers for Disease Control and Prevention report all of their research under the one big category of Life Sciences-Medical Sciences.[17] Within the CDC, research is broken into subgroups, such as infectious diseases and injury prevention, but those categories are too fine-grained for a survey that has to cover the entirety of scientific research in the United States, from agricultural studies to space exploration. As a result, we do not have an accurate picture of the specific projects supported by federal funding.

The second survey, the Survey of Federal Science and Engineering Support to Universities, Colleges, and Nonprofit Institutions (often called the *Federal Support Survey*), asks R&D funding agencies (fifteen federal departments, seventy subagencies, and fifteen independent agencies) to report how much they spent supporting R&D activities by research field. The responses are at best an "educated guess"—partly because it's so difficult to categorize research fields for the reasons described earlier and partly because, for similar reasons, the funding categories themselves differ between the agency internal records and the categories requested by NCSES. So, for example, neither the huge R&D contract spending by the Department of Defense nor that by NASA are reported because they can't separate out spending that is for research from other kinds of spending. In another example, the survey asks agencies to break out spending into basic (making discoveries to advance our understanding of a field) and applied (solving a practical problem) research but the definitions are interpreted differently across agencies so the responses can be quite inaccurate.

Administrative data are not always better. When I was a National Science Foundation (NSF) program officer, we were asked to categorize each grant by how much was basic or applied research. It was impossible to make that determination since discoveries made during the course of basic research can lead to solutions to practical problems, so we generally just reported them as 80 percent basic and 20 percent applied. After a couple of years, we were then told that all NSF research was basic research, so our administrative reporting shifted to 100 percent basic for all grants.

Similarly, if a taxpayer wants to find out what the National Science Foundation or National Institutes of Health (NIH) has funded, she can go onto the NSF or NIH website, and find individual awards. But if she wanted to ask a question such as how much have agencies spent on food safety research, it is impossible to get the answer from querying the websites.[18] And there is almost no public information about the funding levels or the structure and duration of funding for major research agencies like the Department of Defense or the Department of Energy.

Measurement Challenge 2: Who Is Funded
It would be ideal to have information on *who* is funded. Recent academic literature recognizes that people and networks are the

drivers of innovation[19]—and as noted earlier, the NYU economics professor and Nobel Laureate Paul Romer got the prize for pointing out the importance of investing in people and ideas in stimulating economic growth.

There is tantalizing evidence that university R&D does spill over into local economic activity. If you think about the high tech areas around the country, there's usually a major university at the source. In the Boston area for example, there are MIT, Harvard University, and a host of other universities; Silicon Valley has Stanford University and UC Berkeley; the Research Triangle in North Carolina has Duke University, the University of North Carolina, and NC State. And in a more recent example, many attribute the growth of Austin, Texas, in recent decades to the decision to use 1980s oil money to attract some of the top brains in the country to UT Austin. These major examples are important, but we just have not had the large-scale datasets on individuals funded by research to understand the mechanism— which is necessary if we are to learn how and where to invest research dollars better.[20]

But the problem is that surveys cannot capture that information because universities and research funders don't capture structured information about all the people working on research grants. As a result, almost nothing is known about the role of research investments in training key labor inputs, like PhD students, postdocs, and undergraduate students[21]—critical information for both understanding the inputs into the production of science and knowing how many future scientists are in the pipeline. The NIH Office of Extramural Research acknowledged that a working group on the biomedical research workforce was "frustrated and sometimes stymied"[22] by the poor quality of the data available on the biomedical research workforce—there were, for example, major gaps in information on the total number of individuals working as postdocs, inadequate information on postdocs who obtained degrees in other countries, and lack of systematic data on graduate students trained in labs supported by NIH research grants.[23]

In sum, the challenge to measuring who gets funding is that we lack good measures of inputs (all the individuals who are funded) and of the units of analysis (networks, project teams, collaborations). Those data were simply not available—at best, government funders only have data on principal investigators. Information on principal investigators is not linked across agencies, and there is very limited information on those key inputs—postdoctoral students, graduate students, and clinicians.[24]

Measurement Challenge 3: The Results

There is also very limited information about the results of research funding, yielding few answers to questions like: What have we learned about NSF-funded research? What is the economic impact of research funding?[25] It is an article of faith among scientists that science is important and contributes to economic activity, but when they are asked, they resort to important anecdotes like the one about GPS technology resulting from investments in space flights. There is an entire field called scientometrics, which is devoted to studying publications and journal impact factors, but the lack of data means that researchers in the field cannot answer important questions like: What kinds of research programs or institutional structures are most effective? How do investments in R&D translate to more jobs, improved health, and overall societal well-being? How should we balance investments in basic and applied research?[26] New work by researchers such as Massimo Florio are developing frameworks for calculating the costs and benefits of large-scale research initiatives such as the Large Hadron Collider; the data to support that framework have yet to be developed at scale.[27]

Making the Connection: Describing Impact

The challenge, of course, is that it is difficult to describe impact for something as complicated as science, for which there are few empirical linkages and for which it is difficult to establish counterfactual investments. This is one reason why government funding agencies often rely on anecdotes to establish their value, despite the argument that scientists should turn the scientific method on themselves.[28] The NSF routinely cites funding to Larry Page and Sergey Brin to claim credit for Google; the Department of Defense takes credit for developing the internet; the NIH makes much of the value added of the Human Genome Project. The general sense has been that research does not have a clearly defined effect—it is gradual with complex interactions and many confounding factors.[29]

Jack Marburger, the former science adviser to President Bush and head of the Office of Science and Technology Policy, argued that the result of such anecdotal "evidence" is harmful because it means that science as a field is not competitive with other areas that have well-developed methodologies for documenting impact and are more successful in making the case for resources.[30] As Marburger often pointed out, when he attended Cabinet meetings, the Secretary of Transportation had evidence and data showing the impact of investments in highways and roads, the Secretary of Education could show the results of investments in education, and the Congressional Budget Office could run econometric simulations of the impact of changes in funding in almost all areas. In the case of scientific research, however, all Marburger had was anecdotes.

So what should scientists and researchers do to demonstrate their impact? Some agencies in other countries have turned to self-evaluation through commissioned reports. But the results are often not compelling. For example, the European Research Council (ERC) recently released its self-evaluation of frontier research and made the somewhat self-serving claim that "ERC frontier research leaves its mark: 73 percent breakthroughs or major advances."[31] But there are obvious questions when you read the study. How were the funded projects selected? How did funded projects compare to projects that weren't funded? How much did each project spend to generate the breakthrough? Could the money have been better spent elsewhere? Would the scientists have done the work anyway? If the projects were so successful, what can be learned to inform future decisions? Why were there so few failures—shouldn't publicly funded science be riskier than privately funded science? Careful measurement and evaluation look at counterfactuals and selection biases and reflect awareness of what questions are being asked, rather than looking for justification of funding streams.

Agencies in other countries have expended enormous amounts of time and resources in evaluation. The UK Research Councils have developed an impact evaluation approach called the UK Research Excellence Framework, which requires a lot of manual labor. They brought together scientists to evaluate more than seven thousand projects by reading reports produced by the principal investigators and evaluating them in committees. There were four main panels, with thirty-six subpanels, and 1,052 members. The cost of that assessment in 2014 was £250 million—about 2.4 percent of the funding allocated to funding bodies spent over the following six years—and that did not include the cost of the time that scientists spent preparing for the review.[32]

Simply put, bad measurement is wasteful. At best, aggregate measures are uninformative—policy makers still don't know *whether* or *which* research leads to economic growth or better public health—at worst, they are seen as self-serving.

A BETTER APPROACH TO GETTING GOOD DATA AND GOOD MEASUREMENT

It turns out that the story of science measurement has a happy ending, at least in the United States. As it became clear that the federal science agencies were ill equipped to change the system on their own, a new organization—IRIS—emerged.

The story of how this happened is, like the GDP story, one of government identifying a need and pulling academics in to address the need. Jack Marburger at the Office of Science and Technology Policy was frustrated by not knowing the value of investments in scientific research. He twisted arms to fund what would become the National Science Foundation's Science of Science and Innovation Policy (SciSIP) program, designed to develop tools to measure the impacts of scientific research, to assist with decision-making and resource allocation. Roy Weiss, the vice provost for research at the University of Chicago, had attended several Science of Science Policy meetings and was as frustrated as Marburger in the inability of scientists to document the impact of science. The University of Chicago was part of what was then called the Committee for Institutional Cooperation (CIC), a collaborative effort among research universities to pool resources to address common problems. At the request of Roy Weiss, Barbara McFadden Allen, executive director of the CIC, convened a workshop to explore the potential of using new approaches and new data to measure the impact of research funding. Attending the workshop were the researchers and vice provosts for research from the Big Ten schools, and program managers from the Alfred P. Sloan and Ewing Marion Kauffman Foundation.[33] The Sloan and Kauffman program managers were excited enough that they provided seed funding for the establishment of the Institute, which would be led by a dedicated and visionary executive director, Jason Owen-Smith from the University of Michigan. Owen-Smith painstakingly cultivated and validated the necessary organizational and institutional arrangements to establish IRIS. The Institute is governed by member-drafted and ratified bylaws and by a diverse, eminent board of directors comprised of elected and appointed members. The IRIS core facility at the University of Michigan has a staff of fourteen working in teams dedicated to data collection and cleaning, software development, research support and documentation, and administration, including the negotiation and maintenance of memoranda of understanding (MOUs) with data providers and partners.

The Census Bureau has been a key partner at the federal level. It receives transfers of complete IRIS data four times per year to facilitate the integration of UMETRICS with restricted federal datasets that provide comprehensive employment and earnings information for students and researchers in UMET-

RICS together with key employer, demographic, and family characteristics. Census-linked UMETRICS data are made available for research use through the Federal Statistical Research Data Center system. To date, there have been three annual data releases. However, as one would expect given all the organizational issues identified in the previous chapters, the partnership with the Census Bureau has been the most time consuming, slowest, and least transparent of any of the IRIS activities.

IRIS instituted a very innovative organizational approach to draw in more institutions and researchers. It established a set of nodes in addition to the core facility at the University of Michigan and the federal agency partners. The nodes help IRIS expand the research dataset and provide additional access to academic researchers as a source of new ideas, new data, and new products. The nodes are organizations approved by the IRIS board of directors and the University of Michigan Institutional Review Board and are allowed additional access to the restricted data—currently Ohio State University and New York University are approved nodes.

IRIS is like many university centers and think tanks that are dedicated to studying a particular sector of the economy. Executive Director Jason Owen-Smith drew on his experience, and from observing other centers, to build a community of researchers around data and projects. What he has done is essentially provide a data infrastructure that is parallel to and more flexible than the federal statistical system. It is directly responsive to its constituency of research universities in creating useful ways of measuring the scientific and economic impact of their research.

After four years, IRIS has built a data infrastructure that is grounded in transparent, effective governance arrangements and privacy and confidentiality protections, and is supported by a sustainable business model based on contributions from data providers (34 percent of revenue) and sponsored projects (66 percent of revenue). IRIS's flagship contribution is the UMET-RICS dataset introduced at the beginning of this chapter, a growing research resource centered on administrative data from (currently) thirty-one major universities that together account for more than one-third of federal R&D spending in academia. These core data are integrated with a wide variety of information about scientific, educational, and economic outcomes at multiple levels of analysis.

So what does this new organization do differently from the way that the GDP measures were developed and institutionalized? The first difference is the focus on flexible types of data—in particular, transaction data, rather than survey data. Since spending on every funded project can be traced through the human resource and finance systems of each university, IRIS collaborates with universities to draw existing project-level data on those transactions from federally sponsored research to form the UMETRICS dataset infrastructure. This permits researchers to trace the impact of federal science expenditures via purchases of materials and supplies from vendors; support services including financial, IT, and physical space; research services subcontracted to other institutions; and employment of people—the full range of inputs into the production of research. There are three sets of transactions of interest that allow IRIS to trace who is funded.[34] One set of transactions automatically captures information on the people working on each research project, through the HR system of the university. Because there is a charge to the grant when an individual works on it, those charges are captured for every pay period, as is each individual's job title.[35] Another set of transactions automatically captures payments to outside vendors. Any input that is purchased automatically shows up in the financial system in the form of an invoice. This means that information is captured about the type of transaction (object codes), the vendor name and location, and the date and dollar amount of the transaction. The third set of transactions included is subawards—mostly to other academic institutions—with information about the name and location of the subcontracting institution and the amount of the subcontract.

The second difference is the ability to expand using multiple data sources. For example, these data can also be directly linked to the awards that funded them. Rather than rely on one person in an agency filling out a form to "guesstimate" what science is being done and with what results, IRIS researchers use text analysis on grant, publication, and dissertation abstracts to describe the scientific fields. So to describe *what* has been funded at NSF and NIH, researchers use the words scientists themselves use to describe their science and identify topics, just like Google uses the words in text documents to identify topics of interest for web search. The scientific topics can be used to better understand the extent to which a field of research is supported by then linking topics to awards, to identify gaps and trends, and to inform the alignment of research priorities. This information can be used to track the path from research grants to the growth of scientific networks to commercialization of tools. The result is that researchers using IRIS data could uncover new and valuable connections between basic research, applied research, technology development, and technology deployment. It is also notable that linkages are built into the program. For example, the names of people paid on sponsored research projects and information on their year and month of birth are de-identified using hashing technologies and securely assigned unique Protected Identification Keys (PIKs) at the Census Bureau. In this way, the activities of people employed on projects (but not their individual identities) can be linked to the Census Bureau's rich data on employment and employers. The approach provides a privacy-protected way of linking the activities associated with research funding and quantifying the value of the resultant knowledge through the employment outcomes of individuals trained by working on research projects and the nature and performance of the businesses that hire those individuals. In this fashion, the direct links between research funding and economic activity can begin to be unpacked.[36]

The third difference is the very direct connection of IRIS to its user base: research universities. The focus of IRIS is to measure the impact of research. Research universities provide the core data, the baseline funding, and the organizational structure designed to ensure that IRIS produces products that are useful.

IRIS has clearly proven to be a success. There have been many calls for new means to examine and develop evidence-based science and innovation policies[37] and IRIS was recently characterized as a keystone of this emerging field.[38] It is creating new measures and data around graduate STEM (Science, Technology, Engineering, and Mathematics) education, the engineering workforce continuum, the STEM workforce population, data science education and research, regional STEM workforce development, public higher education, evidence-based policy initiatives, team science, and returns to federal investments in research.[39]

It is important to note that the IRIS infrastructure was developed effectively because the mission was clear, a handful of determined people—stakeholders—made it happen, and the organizational structure was carefully designed to succeed. IRIS is a textbook case of how a new institutional framework can be developed that is able to transparently respond to the priorities of key stakeholders, grow flexibly to meet the needs of an expanding multidisciplinary research community, and bring those groups together to determine new directions.

The next chapters will expand on these lessons more generally, with emphasis on the importance of people and mission. They will show how a well-conceived organizational infrastructure could transform the way in which public data are produced.

5 SETTING UP FOR SUCCESS

Nowadays when people have an appointment to go to across town, their calendar app obligingly predicts how long it's going to take to get there. When they go to Amazon to research books that might be of interest, Amazon makes helpful suggestions—and asks for feedback on how to make its platform better. If they select photos from Google Photos, it suggests people to send them to, prompts with other photos it thinks are like the ones selected, and warns if the zip file is going to be especially big. Our apps today are aware of multiple dimensions of the data they manage for us, they update that information in real time, and suggest options and possibilities based upon those dimensions. In other words, the private sector sets itself up for success because it uses data to provide us with useful products and services.

The government—not so much. Lack of data makes Joe Salvo's job much more difficult. He is New York City's chief demographer, and he uses the Census Bureau's American Community Survey (ACS) data to prepare for emergencies like Hurricane Sandy.[1] He needs to use data to decide how to get older residents to physically accessible shelters—operationally, where to tell a fleet of fifty buses to go to pick up and evacuate seniors. He needs data on the characteristics of the local population for the Mayor's Office for People with Disabilities. He needs to identify areas with large senior populations to tell the Metropolitan Transit Authority where to send buses. He needs to identify neighborhoods with significant vulnerable populations so that the Department of Health and Mental Hygiene can install emergency generators at Department of Health facilities. But the products produced by the federal statistical system do not provide him with the value that he needs. The most current data from the prime source about the US population, the ACS, is released two years after collection, and that itself reflects five-year moving averages.

Creating value for the consumer is key to success in the private sector. Chapter 1 included a checklist of eight features of data systems that have made private sector businesses like Amazon and Google successful. The challenge to statistical agencies is figuring out how to get set up for success and produce high-quality data as measured against the same checklist by providing access to data while at the same time protecting privacy and confidentiality.[2]

The problem is that the checklist for agencies is even longer with additional requirements so that Joe Salvo and his counterparts can do their jobs better. One requirement, given that the United States is a democracy, is that statistics should be as unbiased as possible—so that all residents, whatever their characteristics, are counted and that they are treated equally in measurement. Correcting for the inevitable bias in source data is an important role for statistical agencies. Another requirement is that collecting the data is cost-effective, so that the taxpayer gets a good deal. A third requirement is that the information collected is consistent over time so that trends can easily be spotted and responded to. Agencies need outside help from both stakeholders and experts to ensure all these requirements are met. That requires access to data, which requires dealing with confidentiality issues.

The value that is generated when governmental agencies can straightforwardly provide access and produce new measures can be great. For example, the same people who bring you the National Weather service and its weather predictions—the National Oceanic and Atmospheric Agency, or NOAA—have provided scientists and entrepreneurs with access to data to develop new products, such as predicting forest fires and providing real-time intelligence services for natural disasters in the United States and Canada. City transit agencies share transit data with private-sector app developers who produce high-quality apps that offer real-time maps of bus locations and expected arrival times at bus stops and more.[3]

But other cases, when the government has confidential data, which is the case for most statistical agencies, are different. We need to be able to rely on our government to keep some data very private, but that will often mean that we have to give up on the granularity of government data that are produced. If, for example, the IRS provided so much information about taxpayers that it was possible to know how much money a given individual made, the public would be outraged.

So many government agencies have to worry about two things: (1) producing data that have value and (2) at the same time ensuring that the confidentiality of data owners is protected. This can be done. Some—smaller—governments have succeeded better than others in creating data systems that live up to the checklist of the desired features while at the same time protecting privacy.

Take the child services system as an example. To put child services in context, almost four in ten US children will be referred to their local government for possible child abuse or neglect by the time they're eighteen.[4] That's almost four million referrals a year. Frontline caseworkers have to make quick decisions on these referrals. If they are wrong in either direction, the potential downside is enormous: Children incorrectly screened because of inadequate or inaccurate data could be ripped away from loving families.[5] Or, conversely, also as a result of poor data, children could be left with abusive families and die.[6] Furthermore, there could be bias in decisions, leaving black or LGBTQ parents more likely to be penalized, for example.

In 2014, Allegheny County's Office of Children, Youth and Families (CYF) in Pennsylvania stepped up to the plate to use its internal data in a careful and ethical manner to help caseworkers do their job better. The results have captured national attention, as reported in a *New York Times Magazine* article.[7] CYF brought in academic experts to design an automatic risk-scoring tool that summarizes information about a family to help the caseworker make better decisions. The risk score, a number between 1 and 20, makes use of a great deal of the information about the family in the county's system, such as child welfare records, jail records, and behavioral health records, to predict adverse events that can lead to placing a child in foster care.

An analysis of the effectiveness of that tool showed that a child whose placement score at referral is the highest possible— 20—is twenty-one times more likely to be admitted to a hospital for a self-inflicted injury, seventeen times more likely to be admitted for being physically assaulted, and 1.4 times more likely to be admitted for suffering from an accidental fall than a child with a risk score of 1, the lowest possible. An independent evaluation found that caseworker decisions that were informed by the score were more accurate (cases were more likely to be correctly identified as needing help and less likely to be incorrectly identified as not needing help), case workloads decreased, and racial bias was likely to be reduced.[8] On the eight-item checklist Allegheny County hit on all items. They produced a new product that was used, was cost effective, and produced real-time, accurate, complete, relevant, accessible, interpretable, granular, and consistent data. And CYF didn't breach confidentiality. But most importantly, Allegheny County worked carefully and openly with advocates for parents, children, and civil rights to ensure that the program was not built behind closed doors. They worked, in other words, to ensure that the new measures were democratically developed and used.

The Allegheny County story is one illustration of how new technologies can be used to democratize the decision of how to balance the ever-present tradeoff between the utility of new measurement against the risk of compromising confidentiality. They took advantage of the potential to create useful information that people and policy makers need while at the same time protecting privacy. That potential can be made real in other contexts by making the value of data clearer to the public. While that utility/cost tradeoff has typically been made by a small group of experts within an agency, there are many new tools that can democratize the decision by providing more information to the public. This chapter goes into more detail about the challenges of and new approaches to the utility/cost tradeoff. There are many lessons to be learned from past experiences.

CREATING VALUE AND PROTECTING CONFIDENTIALITY

In the late 1990s, I worked with federal, state, and local government agencies to develop a new statistical program.[9] Turgidly named the Longitudinal Employer-Household Dynamics (LEHD) program, it is now a major resource for workforce and transportation planners—as well as the scientific community. LEHD succeeded because we figured out how to combine existing data to create new, valuable products while protecting confidentiality.

LEHD started out as a research project[10] to estimate the returns to on-the-job training. There had been a lot of work done on the returns to formal education, which mostly ends when people are eighteen to twenty years old, but much less on the returns to on-the-job training that are really important for both firms and workers throughout their worklives. Part of the reason we know so little about this is that you need representative data on both firms (who get some of the returns to on-the-job training through increased worker productivity) and workers (who get the rest of the returns through increased earnings); those data are confidential and difficult to access.

What many of us started to realize as we began to work with the data was that it was possible to create even more value than simply looking at the returns to training. My research project could be turned into a way of combining then-new types of data (administrative records generated from the administration of government programs) to create linked employer-employee data and generate a fundamentally new set of measures of jobs and the dynamic interactions of workers and firms over time.[11] Entirely new measures of workforce dynamics were created—in particular, new measures of workforce churn, that is, workers' movements across firms and industries. Those same data, matched to other records with careful confidentiality protections, could be used to produce detailed aggregated information about where jobs were as well as what the earnings levels were for people hired and for people currently employed—with breakouts by age, sex, race, and education groups.

This simple research project on job flows, worker flows, and churning[12] turned into four new national data series that have democratized data for many people and businesses who otherwise would not have access to such information. The very first series, which we called the Quarterly Workforce Indicators, is used by workforce boards (a network of offices supported by federal, state, and local agencies charged with helping local residents find jobs or advance in their careers) to make better evidence-based decisions about what training to provide where. This is because the thirty-two indicators in the series provide detailed information about the earnings of new hires and the number of stable jobs in each industry in their local area (city, county, or workforce area). Small businesses also have access to this data series so they can have information about the going pay for people in their area, which gives them a more equal footing with the big firms that can pay human resource companies to provide such data.

The second data series is showcased in a graphical and data tool, which we called On-The-Map. The tool provides urban planners, chambers of commerce, and small businesses making location decisions with summary information about how many people live and work at an even more detailed level of geography (the block level) and their demographic characteristics. The third data series, Job-to-Job Flows, is a set of statistics on job mobility such as "job-to-job transition rates, hires and separations to and from employment, earnings changes due to job change, and the characteristics of origin and destination jobs for job-to-job transitions."[13] It thus provides state governments with important information about inter-industry and interstate worker flows. The latest data series has just started up, and combines LEHD data with state-level post-secondary school data to create a series called Post Secondary Employment Outcomes so that students have a better sense of the earnings and employment outcomes in different fields. All the data series are used by thousands of organizations—chambers of commerce, economic development agencies, transportation planners, and urban planners all across the country, and they are a staple of many urban planning classes in universities.

Even better, the cost of this project was tiny: because existing data were being reused, the cost per record was cents rather than the many hundreds of dollars it costs to get a response from each survey respondent.

So how did these new data and set of measures get created? Essentially, this project was demand driven—demand from the Census Bureau, state agencies, particularly state Departments of Labor and academics (John Abowd at Cornell University, John Haltiwanger at the University of Maryland and also chief economist at the Census Bureau, and me in my former position as a professor at American University).[14]

The Census Bureau staff had had many discussions about how to link the two sides of economic activity—workers and firms, whose characteristics they had captured largely through surveys—and could not figure out how to use survey data to do so. I had access to state-level administrative data that captured the links between firms and workers, but I had no information about the characteristics of either. A colleague of mine at the Census Bureau, Nancy Gordon, brought me in as an American Statistical Association/National Science Foundation fellow to see if it was possible to combine the administrative data with the Census Bureau data. A year later, John Abowd joined the team.[15] In parallel, state labor market agencies were looking for more information to help support their local workforce boards responsible for training workers for available jobs.

The story is similar (although at a much humbler level) to how GDP came to be. That is, during the Great Depression, the government needed to get new data and measures created; they reached out to the NBER and brought in academic experts and provided them with access to data. In the case of LEHD, the Census Bureau had talked about the value of linked employer-employee data and reached out to me to see if it was possible to build such an infrastructure. Even with high-level support, we found that it is overwhelmingly difficult to incentivize bureaucracy to turn good ideas into operational procedures.[16] In our case, there were enormous hurdles to overcome—bureaucratic inertia, incredible turf battles, lack of funding and resources—and of course privacy concerns.

The way we overcame the hurdles was that we were able to make the case for the utility of the data while at the same time protecting confidentiality. The bureaucratic inertia was at least partly overcome by finding good colleagues to work with, as discussed in chapter 6. The confidentiality protections offered by the federal statistical community were also important—clearly without privacy protections it is impossible to access confidential data. Since federal agencies had historically been able to invest in big, secure IT infrastructures, and had a workforce skilled in working with large-scale data, the federal agencies were the logical place to host the data.

That was twenty years ago. The situation has now changed with new technologies, including greater understanding of how to protect privacy; the advent of secure cloud computing; and a new workforce with new skills, notably increasing numbers of trained computer scientists outside statistical agencies who have new techniques and tools to manage large-scale data resources.[17] It is possible to democratize the data even further by providing those tools and approaches that permit more access and produce more value.

SETTING UP ACCESS

Protecting privacy is a paramount concern in data collection. But it is also clear that citizens are aware of the tradeoff between privacy and utility, particularly if the tradeoff is explained. In a recent report commissioned by the Data Funders Collaborative, the consulting firm Topos reported a private citizen saying, "I think in our current world we have to be concerned about data security. There are too many breaches not to be concerned. But I can absolutely see how social services having access to a child's school and health records could keep a child safer and maybe save a life."[18] This quote encapsulates the lessons learned in the

Allegheny County example, where the county worked with its constituents to make better use of data to allocate resources and better protect children.

Allowing access to confidential data—which is the data on individuals and businesses that is necessary to generate the measures required of most statistical agencies—is hard, because it's necessary to ensure that individuals and organizations cannot be reidentified. This is quite a challenge—simple information like zip code, date of birth, and sex can be sufficient to reidentify nine out of ten Americans.[19] Even a decade ago, individual browsing habits—without any other identifiers—were used to find out an AOL user's identity.[20] And in 2016, the *New York Times Magazine* reported that no more information was needed by Target than a sixteen-year-old's shopping habits to find out that she was pregnant before her father even knew.[21]

An important historical approach to keeping data safe has been to allow access only onsite at federal agencies or designated secure centers.[22] The idea was that an authorized agency representative could then oversee researchers as they physically sat in a secure environment. Although the approach has been successful in expanding access to federal data for scientists, it tends to favor larger, wealthier universities and researchers who are able to travel to a physical center to do their work. The access is largely to federal agency data, not to the state or local data that are often essential for decision-making, or the increasingly relevant new types of data (retail scanner, sensor, cell phone or social media). Such inadequate access has effectively limited innovation. However, this limitation can be made less stringent by using new technology to create better access while protecting privacy by following what is referred to as the "five safes" framework: safe projects, safe people, safe settings, safe data, and safe outputs.[23]

Technology can help with addressing the first "safe": "safe projects." A safe project creates value for the agency and the people it serves and is consistent with current legal, policy, ethical, and other relevant restrictions. In other words, the starting point is to ensure that a project has utility. Without that utility, no data access occurs. Once a safe project is identified and agreed to, the people who are authorized to access the data for those purposes are identified, the datasets are defined, and the protocols for protecting the data are also agreed to. The rules can be encoded and tracked at a project level for the next "safe"— safe people.

The second "safe" is about reducing the risk to privacy of individual access and increasing the likely value of that access by ensuring that access is restricted to trusted people. It requires that the agencies responsible for the data—the data owners— ensure that only authorized people (often referred to as "safe people") have access to the agency data. The requirements for authorization could be in the form of training and certifications, as well as background investigations and other protections such as signing legal agreements, confidentiality pledges, and providing employer indemnification in case of a breach. New technology can be used to automate those access rules and make them more transparent. Automated tools have been developed that can clarify the relevant steps both for those who request data access and for those who determine whether to grant or reject that access. These functions are essential in that they provide necessary controls while also enabling straightforward answers to critical questions such as "Which projects use my data?" or

"How is my data being used and which byproducts were generated by whom?"—and they enable those answers to be made public in a democratic way.

The third "safe" is establishing a safe environment within which confidential data can be accessed—this is often referred to as a "safe setting." Because cloud computing is now both secure and affordable, it is possible to create a secure environment that can be continuously monitored by the data steward—the individual designated by the agency to be responsible for protecting privacy—who can ensure that the rules are being followed for each project. The federal government has set up a program called FedRAMP (https://fedramp.gov) to provide a standardized checklist that data owners, particularly federal agencies, can use to ensure that approved practices (like identity management, continuous monitoring, encryption, and training) are adhered to by data users and that agencies can have their own cloud-based secure environment with established access boundaries, so that no data can come into or out of the environment without approval. FedRAMP also has an infrastructure of certified external assessment organizations to verify that appropriate security is in place. There are more than four hundred different controls that are monitored, including user training, audit logs, identity management, and incident response protocols.

The fourth "safe" is the de-identification of data to ensure what is often referred to as "safe data." Statistical methods may be applied to de-identify data and minimize disclosure and reidentification for each project, person, and setting. An entire subfield of computer science has developed ways of ensuring that personal identifiers such as name and social security number are almost impossible to unpack. A cryptographic approach—the

HMAC (Hashed Message Authentication Code)—is a standard way of sharing this sensitive information.[24]

The fifth "safe" is to minimize the risk that individuals can get reidentified from the results of the analysis by ensuring what is known as "safe output." Here again, the technology has also advanced to a stage where data owners can set their own requirements to constrain what analytical results can be released from the environment[25]—although it's worth noting that the scientific basis for release is an area of huge debate.[26] The Liberty Island example cited in chapter 2 is an example of protecting data in a way that negatively affects data quality. Building an arsenal of information about how much to trade off the data quality associated with valuable projects (the utility associated with data access) deserves its own discussion.

SETTING UP VALUE

Most agencies are very aware that they could serve their customers more effectively, at lower cost, and in new ways if the agencies could make more use of their existing data. And if agencies were able to provide information to their stakeholders about the value of data use, the agencies could justify more access, improve measurement, and produce new products. Unfortunately, what often happens is that the agencies will allow access, and researchers will do research, publish it two years later, and then not report the results back. There are manual follow-ups, but inevitably much of the value gets lost simply because it's so hard to keep track of what's been done with the data. This is particularly unfortunate because authors of research publications tend to become expert in the use of particular datasets and their adjacent topics. Agencies could use that knowledge to identify the research efforts that benefit from their datasets, as well as policy related to that published research, and who the top experts—the brain trust—are for adjacent topics, and how to reach them. And as agencies provide more information about the value of data, their constituents can make a more informed decision about whether the investment in data has been worth the cost—a key component of democratic decision-making.

Building a platform that can provide this information about the value of research outputs from various government datasets is technologically feasible. We see a multitude of examples of successful platforms in the private sector. It used to be that if I wanted to find out what books had been written on a particular topic, I would have to go to the local bookstore and find an employee who had read similar books and get recommendations. Or I would talk to a research librarian at an academic library who would have more robust cataloging tools to refer to. Now, platforms like Amazon empower users to search and discover new products and services and report back on their quality. A similar platform could be developed for data so that agencies could find what work had been done using their data, who else had done similar work, what results had been generated, and what other similar datasets had been used. Then the public would be able to see the value of public data and to find information relevant to each user's needs and interests.

So, for example, suppose that Joe Salvo wanted to know what datasets—other than the American Community Survey—were available to figure out where to send his buses to evacuate seniors in a weather emergency. He could type in his request and it might pop up other datasets—based, say, on 311 data, cell phone data, retail scanner data, or any other information that has been collected for other purposes—that could be repurposed for his use. In terms of our checklist, the other measures of quality—like timeliness, cost, accessibility, and granularity—might be more important to him, and he could see how other users like him in other cities had used and rated the data.

The private sector has been building platforms that search, recommend, and rank for over a decade. We know how to build them—the challenge here is repurposing the knowledge to rate and reuse data.

There are quite a few moving parts, but the basics of how to automate the development of these knowledge bases are not a dark art. The main steps are as follows.

First, develop a body of research articles that sufficiently represents the population of all documents that use research datasets, and identify the datasets in that corpus. This first step is quite manual. The datasets need to be tagged so they can be found in the subsequent steps. Creating a good tag is time consuming and expensive,[27] but it pays off in the reliability and comprehensiveness of the knowledge base that results from it. So, for example, take a piece I wrote with my coauthors using the UMETRICS dataset described in chapter 4.[28] In that article, we say "we combine data from the UMETRICS project, which provided administrative records on graduate students supported on funded research, with data from the U.S. Bureau of the Census." The tag would say "UMETRICS" and "data from the US Bureau of the Census" so that the machine learning algorithm would know the sources of data used in our research.

The second step is to develop a common understanding of the types of data in those datasets, how the data relates to other data, and how those types and their relationships can be unambiguously expressed so that computers can know how to put the pieces together. This framework is called an "ontology." To take an oversimplified example, the datasets in a corpus of chemical research often have data about atoms, molecules, atomic weights, types of bonds, and more. An ontology would have standard terminology for each of those, and would understand that atoms make up molecules, but molecules never make up atoms, and that atoms have weights, but chemical bonds do not—and so on. Developing a standard ontology irons out the differences in how each of these individual datasets may express that information, enabling a computer to find information more reliably, and to notice relationships among the many different sets of data.

Developing a standard ontology is not a trivial task. It is in fact a fundamental scientific problem, and one that is often in the domain of expert librarians and information scientists. And because the world is messy, ontologies are unlikely to ever be complete or to capture all possible information. Yet, even modest ontologies that minimally control the vocabulary researchers use would have important benefits. Larger efforts have their own payoffs and tradeoffs. For example, the Data Documentation Initiative (DDI) provides a machine-actionable generic specification for describing surveys and other observational data, and is actively used by many statistical agencies and academic data repositories.[29] But, DDI was developed for observational data, which is just one type of scientific data. And the generality of DDI also means that it loses much of what's specific to subdomains of social science. Designing systems that work at both a more abstract level that covers multiple fields without losing what is specific to subdisciplines is a difficult challenge, but one entirely worth addressing.

The third step: to automate the development of knowledge bases and to improve and scale the manual tagging in the first step, we need to be able to automate the identification and extraction of the names of datasets from the articles in the corpus. Some approaches have essentially relied on constructing massive lists—a registry—of the sorts of words and names typically found in datasets in a particular field. So, for example, you need to link the term "American Community Survey" with "Am. Comm. Surv." with "ACS." But this means datasets that happen not to use those entities named in those ways will be missed. It also requires keeping the list up to date as research evolves.

A more sophisticated approach builds models of the semantic context within which these datasets occurred, basically trying to understand that context not through the particular words used but by what the words *mean*. So in the preceding example, the language around the snippet "provided administrative records on graduate students supported on funded research, with data from the U.S. Bureau of the Census" acts as a signal to the algorithm that the author is talking about data. When successful, this approach can also tell us about related datasets—just as Amazon knows what other books you might be interested in based on the purchasing habits of people just like you. The algorithms can yield clusters of datasets with some sense of what they might mean to human searchers and how these clusters relate, so the system can find datasets based on how users refer to them, rather than only replying to searches with the datasets that use the exact words in the user's query.[30] For example, knowing that the same researcher used Dataset A on educational attainment and Dataset B on labor market outcomes would suggest a relationship between Datasets A and B that would not necessarily be understood by looking at the topics alone.

Then, the fourth step is to develop a recommender engine—so that instead of Joe Salvo getting a laundry list of possible datasets, he gets ones that are customized to his particular interests. It's that recommender engine on Amazon that has been an important part of its success. Imagine building a recommender engine for Joe Salvo based on the "best" information about fields, experts, related datasets, and useful publications. That recommender engine is built on what's called knowledge graphs: these link concepts, their descriptions, contextual correlations, relationships with authors and venues, and relationships learned programmatically from the graph structure. An active community has been attempting to build recommendation engines so researchers can find papers without digging through irrelevant information.[31] The ResearchGate platform, for example, is brilliant at suggesting papers that you might be interested in based on your work and the work of your coauthors.

The fifth step is engaging users who provide feedback and validation of the graph's suggestions so it can be tuned. Online platforms that effectively meet this challenge have a number of common features: they typically provide clear visual feedback, and a sense that one is contributing to a communal enterprise, following even minor user interactions, and they reward increased user engagement with new abilities, community feedback, and/or greater visibility. Take, for example, data.world, which is a data catalog that uses a knowledge graph to map data to business concepts. On StackOverflow, an open community for coders to ask and answer questions, users gain a range of editorial powers (e.g., the ability to edit others' answers) as their user score increases. And on GitHub, where people can share code, the authors of highly starred repositories gain in reputation and exposure, often leading to new career opportunities.

Arguably the most general common feature of such systems is that they work hard to align individual and communal incentives to ensure that what's good for an individual user is also good for the entire community. When such an alignment is absent—as is regrettably often the case in social science research—individuals may continue to behave in ways that harm the collective endeavor. Since research datasets generally have not been thought of as primary research outputs, there is an endemic inconsistency when referencing datasets in research work. This makes it difficult to know not only in which studies particular datasets have been used or reused, but also the context and impact of their use.

In sum, the technology exists to develop automated quality metrics. It is possible to develop and sustain a large-scale, continuously learning engine that automatically encodes and makes available every data product and develops measures of access and use. The data community would then have a working set of quality metrics that is continuously improved by the efforts both of the experts who maintain it and the users who interact with it—providing better and better recommendations and measuring the value of data based on externally validated metrics.

A PRAGMATIC APPROACH

In the Topos partnership's report cited earlier, the people Topos talked to made it clear that access to data had to be tied to the value that came from it. Topos cites one person as saying,

> I think it is important to share information. One agency could be learning something very valuable that another group could benefit from, but has no knowledge of. . . . The benefits could be in the form of programs. For example, local health agency has good findings. They partner with a school to implement a program to benefit the area's youth. Suicide prevention is a really big topic right now. That would be a topic area where this could benefit.[32]

The good news is that new legislation has established a possible way forward. The Foundations of Evidence-Based Policymaking Act requires that each statistical agency must produce and disseminate relevant, accurate, objective, and timely data, as well as ensure that the data are used only for statistical purposes and that the confidentiality of the data is protected.

The Evidence Act and the Federal Data Strategy also now require all government agencies to identify data needs to answer priority agency questions, and to post inventories of their data assets. So the data platform, or family of data platforms, could have access that is tied to the value that is expected to be generated. Multiple tiers could be established, with greater access for an analyst directly tied to how much value the analyst would produce as a result of that access. Such a tiered system would demonstrate to the public the value of providing greater access to data, and reward agencies and researchers for providing that access if it creates more value. In other words, as individuals demonstrate that they have provided more utility to the public as a result of their access—as in the Allegheny County example, or the LEHD example—they can be provided with greater access so that they can provide even more utility in the future.

A possible method of tiering access is based on the "five safes" approach to privacy described earlier in this chapter. The qualifications of each tier should be objective and publicly announced so that the public is aware of the tradeoff:

Safe Projects. As discussed in this chapter, safe projects are those that have value to the community served by the agency—projects cannot just be about anything. Agencies could post a categorization of the value to the public of their products based on automated quality metrics such as community use of data, reuse of existing data, reproducibility of analysis, and providing not just the data but also the contextual information that makes them useful, such as the methodologies employed.

Safe People. Organizations could develop a tiered approach to who gets access to this data. Since the aim is to enable the continuous improvement of the data, qualifications could include academic degrees, or experience such as prior work with the agency and prior research on topics of interest to the agency. Also, previous contributions to data quality should count; these could include dataset documentation, codebook publication, or published research. Individuals or organizations who show greater contributions to data quality would be permitted greater access.

Safe Settings. Organizations could provide different levels of access based on the sensitivity of the data and the potential gains from access.

Safe Data and Safe Output. Organizations could offer access to data of differing degrees of quality based on the credentials of the individual—how much that individual is trusted. The most valuable data would be original files, followed by de-identified personal information that has been protected by digital techniques such as hash algorithms. We've already discussed the problems associated with data protection (the Liberty Island example), but if users understood the downside and were able to adjust for the problems, they could be provided access to such files. And many users are perfectly happy with summary tables that answer questions like "how many people over 65 live in New York City"—so new publicly useful indicators could be generated from the most restricted data by expert data scientists.

This legislation is just the beginning. It doesn't provide a road map forward, but the steps outlined in this chapter do. As we have argued, the ultimate goal of a new data system is to create new data that are useful. People—like students, small businesses, planners—need a toolkit—like a platform or set of platforms—that can be used, in the words of the Topos partnership report, "to learn about their data that's being shared and have a say in who can see it and what it can be used for."[33] Chapters 6 and 7 describe the people that are necessary to achieve the vision and the organizational structure that could make it happen.

6 ESTABLISHING THE FOUNDATION

The foundation of success for any organization is creating value. The challenge for public agencies is knowing how to do so. I believe the key is building a foundation that creates links between those insiders who know how to get things done and outsiders who have ideas about what can be done. The insiders are the public servants who are the vectors of change in any bureaucracy. Change cannot happen without their buy-in. This is particularly true for state and local government agencies—their staff are closest to understanding the needs of their constituencies and they know the strengths and weaknesses of the data their agencies generate. The outsiders are often academic researchers, who have the tools and skill sets to develop new products. In Allegheny County's Office of Children, Youth and Families, for example, the case management indicators would have gone nowhere if frontline staff had not been engaged from the beginning; if the design had not been structured to ensure that the external researchers helped, not hindered, the frontline staff; and if the frontline staff had not been allowed to override the existing model. The outside researchers were critical to providing the technical capacity to build new tools and approaches.

In the Longitudinal Employer Household Dynamics (LEHD) program cited in chapter 5, insiders and outsiders were critical. Our team of academics created new data that have had enormous value, but we would have failed miserably without incredibly dedicated public servants—largely in the state agencies, but also in the federal agencies—who effected change. Two of the most influential were Henry Jackson and George Putnam, the director and deputy director of Labor Market Information from the Illinois Department of Employment Security. They were essential catalysts of change in creating the program that transformed the data landscape for their agency and their sister employment agencies across the country.

This chapter will spell out why Putnam and Jackson, and others like them, were so important in identifying the value that ensured the LEHD program's success over the past twenty years, and why both insiders and outsiders were necessary to create that value. The lessons are simple and in some ways old-fashioned, but are validated by many, many experts.[1]

Knowing what products have value, as discussed in chapter 5, is dependent on the people in the agencies who know what has value to the people they serve. Right now, the barriers are high when a public sector worker presents a new idea about how data can be put to work. There are usually many legal and technical hurdles to clear. There are so few prototype successes to point to. Rewards are few, and there can be huge penalties for failure.[2]

And there are many forces pushing back against change. The pressures to meet existing program needs make it difficult for agencies to try anything new, much less to create organized pipelines of new products. Government salary structures make it difficult to hire and retain enough in-house data analysts. For example, it is not unusual for experienced data scientists hired by Google, Amazon, Microsoft, or Facebook to be paid more than $300,000, plus stock options and generous bonuses. In contrast, the salary cap for a top level nonmanagerial government employee is around $140,000, with minimal bonuses (although there is a cost of living adjustment for those living in expensive areas). It can also be demoralizing to work in the federal government with constrained or uncertain budgets and shutdown threats.

These combined challenges have led to the current negative loop: agencies cannot get the resources necessary to make use of new data, and because they don't use new data, they don't get new resources.

Creating value is hard work too. It's hard for agency staff to build useful products from the new types of data—just as hard as it is for agency staff to create indicators from the survey data described in chapter 2. Jeff Liebman, who runs Harvard University's Government Performance Lab, uses a very specific example to make the point. Suppose a state wants to use data and indicators to reduce infant mortality and the number of low-birthweight births.[3] First, the state needs to look at infant deaths and low-birthweight births to identify the entire target population and understand the issues. Liebman says the state agency then needs to answer questions such as: Where are the geographic hot spots? What fraction of the mothers are teens, smokers, drug or alcohol abusers, overweight, or undernourished? These data might need to come from birth records, Medicaid claims data, or medical charts. Then the state needs to use data on risk levels and intervention cost effectiveness for specific subpopulations so that the right people are referred to the right services. There are many options with different costs and different effectiveness. Home visits can be important—should they involve a lengthy in-person visit or should they be just a quick check in? Community public health campaigns can also be effective, so should limited resources be allocated to encouraging better nutrition, exercise, or healthy infant sleep practices—or all three? Or should resources be allocated to drug treatment programs and teen pregnancy prevention?

Then the state has to monitor the effectiveness of any program—track the receipt of services and work with service providers to ensure that people don't fall through the cracks. Indicators could be developed that show the percentage of pregnant mothers referred to home visiting who actually received services. The state then needs to annually compare outcomes for individuals referred to different services to make decisions about how to allocate resources and adjust referral models going forward. If the measures aren't well defined, and data aren't part of service delivery, money would be wasted and outcomes for vulnerable populations would not improve. As Liebman says, "We need to use data and analysis throughout the policymaking and service delivery chain to drive the systems re-engineering and continuous improvement efforts necessary to achieve better outcomes."[4]

INSIDERS AND OUTSIDERS

In the case of the LEHD program, value creation came from both insiders and outsiders.

I was the outsider. I was granted a Census Bureau fellowship (established by the American Statistical Association and the

National Science Foundation) originally to work on a simple pilot research project as mentioned in chapter 5: I was going to use data from the state of Maryland and link it to Census Bureau data to create an employer-employee dataset so we and others could study the return on investment for on-the-job training. The Census Bureau also viewed this as an experiment to see if it was feasible to integrate data from multiple sources, each collected in its own way and with its own idiosyncrasies. The Census Bureau and the Bureau of Labor Statistics, which also became interested in the project, supported a team of four (including me) to do the pilot.

It's worth digressing a bit to discuss how hard it is to combine administrative data—and why it is so important to have motivated and skilled civil servants working on the problem.

The first challenge is figuring out what data are needed, as Liebman pointed out, and then getting permission to work with the data.[5] As noted in chapter 2, permission can take years.

Another challenge is simply combining data from different sources with different identifiers. To get a sense of how hard it is, just think how many different ways your name is spelled in mailings that come to your home. This is often called the *entity resolution* or *disambiguation* problem[6]—figuring out whether someone in their files called Javier Martinez is the same person as a person in a file from another agency called Havier Marteenez (which happens with surprising frequency). The costs of merging the two files incorrectly are low if you're sending out mailings, but they're high if an agency is trying to do a survey. If the files are incorrectly merged to say that Javier and Havier are the same person when they are different, and they are both Hispanic, the number of Hispanics will be undercounted because the two data points will be combined to be one in the final file. If the files are incorrectly merged to say they are different people when they are the same, the result will be to overcount Hispanics because what is really one data point will be counted as two. It's important not only to count people (so that they count), but to ensure that counts are accurate.

A third challenge is building consistency when categories change over time, such as an industrial classification. Although it doesn't happen as much as it should (see those hundreds of agricultural categories still kicking around), some industry categories do change to recognize the fact that businesses are producing very different goods and services than they did before. When this happens, it substantially affects estimates of employment measures. For example, if the change in classifications isn't accounted for, the Bureau of Labor Statistics estimates that US manufacturing employment dropped 18 percent from March 2001 to March 2007; if classification change is accounted for, however, then the decline is 15.4 percent—a difference of more than four hundred thousand manufacturing jobs.[7] Experts reckon that building a clean analytical dataset takes 80–90 percent of the time spent on an analytical project.[8]

Before the work of combining the data can begin, however, a researcher must gain access to the data, and that requires permission and trust. In the case of the LEHD program, getting the permissions depended on the trust that my dissertation advisor had built up with the State of Maryland and the championing of the project by Nancy Gordon, the associate director of demographic programs at the Census Bureau.[9] Building the links between the Maryland data and the federal datasets was time-consuming work that took over a year of the team's time.[10]

We established value to the Census Bureau by running a large-scale conference[11] that demonstrated to the federal agencies that other countries had created value from linking data, while protecting confidentiality. Once we had established that the approach was indeed feasible, my fellowship was expanded and continued to see if we could build an infrastructure based on the reuse and repurposing of existing data to build new indicators, and an additional fellow was brought on board. I made a presentation about the project to the national meeting of the state Departments of Labor, and several states, primarily the state of Illinois, namely Henry Jackson and George Putnam, expressed interest in becoming involved.

The success of the fellowships in establishing LEHD highlights the importance of bringing in new blood[12]—or, as the physicist Robert Oppenheimer once noted, "the best way to transmit knowledge is to wrap it up in a human being."[13] But having outsiders is only part of the story. The outsiders need to take time to get insiders used to the ideas, to figure out how to create value from them and to address many of the bureaucratic issues I have highlighted.

The insiders were Jackson and Putnam. We outside academics were thrilled at the potential to generate new labor market measures in their own right. Jackson and Putnam could see how they could be used to create value for their constituencies—particularly workforce boards who served both employers and workers looking for jobs. They guided us into developing the measures that had the most value. And they were able to leverage connections through their agency, the Illinois Department of Employment Security, to share what they were learning not only with other Illinois agencies, but also at the national level through connections with networks that connected state agencies.

Insiders and outsiders were thus able to build and design a series of new products that are now used by thousands of urban planners, transportation planners, scholars, and workforce boards throughout the country. "Good research" in this space is a union of interests on both sides, facilitated by the collaboration of insiders and outsiders

There are institutional ways of bringing in outsiders to establish ongoing face-to-face contacts. Fellowships can be an important element—that is how I was brought in. Many philanthropic foundations support embedded data scientists who come in and work in agencies and help develop capacity to solve problems. For example, there's a not-for-profit organization called Govern for America that has set up two-year fellowships for recent graduates within state agencies.

THE IMPORTANCE OF CREATING VALUE

As discussed earlier, the use of data has changed business operations. Facebook, Google, Microsoft, Amazon, and Apple, the five largest companies in the United States, create value very differently from the General Electrics and General Motors of twenty or thirty years ago.[14] But the use of data for businesses only makes sense if it helps them, directly or indirectly, to sell their products and services.

Public agencies obviously don't rely on selling anything to customers. Nevertheless, their customers—like the workforce boards, employers, and training organizations that used the LEHD data to improve on-the-job training programs—are the agencies' lifeline, just as customers are for businesses. When I ask Jackson and Putnam—and the many other public servants with whom I've worked—why they stepped up to the plate to work with me to get LEHD started, they say something like "because it created value for our customers." Or sometimes they'll say, "It's just good government" the way a businessperson might say, "It's just good business." Indeed, I have found very similar mindsets shared by government and business folk in this focus on value.

Agencies, however, don't always immediately see the value that can be wrung from data. So when talking with their representatives, it's important not only to describe what the new products are, but also to explain how those products can help them in their missions. For example, Unemployment Insurance Wage Records could be used to produce new measures of the jobs that were being created for people of specific ages and education, broken down by detailed industry and geographic location. The Quarterly Workforce Indicators product (QWI) that I discussed in chapter 5 created value because it enabled workforce boards to provide information to training programs that could help them evaluate the jobs available for trainees in the local area. The Quarterly Workforce Indicators would give workers information about what they could expect to earn. QWI would enable firms to know the going market rate for workers in their labor pool. Describing the value LEHD could bring to workforce boards, workers, and employers helped agencies to get on board with the program. Understanding the different constituencies to whom LEHD would bring value helped the agencies to fine-tune the development of the most useful indicators, and made it easier to get elected officials on board as well.

The lesson is that data do not have value in their own right. Data only have value if they can be used to create products that have value to the agencies and, directly or indirectly, to the customers the agencies serve. That requires capable people in those agencies who have both the technical skills to work with the data and the understanding of what is needed.

LOOKING AHEAD

Building the LEHD program required visits to almost every state in the country to develop ideas for products that had value. In the early years, as I mentioned in chapter 5, the states drove the creation of the Quarterly Workforce Indicators, which provided new information about earnings and employment at the level of county, metro area, and the geographic units served by local workforce boards. State labor market agencies could do that not only because they understood their constituencies (the workforce boards and the citizens of their states) better but also because they understood how the data were generated. In my view, a successful foundation will require building workforce capacity and access to data *at the state and local level* and will be one of the most promising ways to continuously innovate and generate new measures.

Building that skill set is hard, as Liebman pointed out— the data are difficult to work with, it's hard to link data across agency lines, and it's hard to share results. But the opportunity now exists to do so. In 2016, then Speaker of the House Congressman Paul Ryan of Wisconsin and Senator Patty Murray of Washington established the US Commission on Evidence-Based Policymaking[15] with the goal of getting experts to recommend ways to bring together data to inform policy. As the commission report noted, "Policymakers must have good information on which to base their decisions about improving the viability and effectiveness of government programs and policies. Today, too little evidence is produced to meet this need."[16]

My colleagues and I were asked to build a secure platform that could host confidential administrative data and, by showing how it could be done, inform the decision-making of the commission. The lessons from both the LEHD program and the Institute for Research on Innovation and Science were clear. A completely different approach to data collection and integration as well as the creation of new measures were critical. Putting data in the secure platform was necessary but not sufficient. Improving the ability of governmental agencies to develop and implement changes in how they collect and use data is not just about overcoming bureaucratic inertia[17]—it requires rethinking the way in which the agencies do their jobs.

The initial remit that we were given was to demonstrate that an "administrative records clearing house" could be built. But that remit didn't consider that the government agencies needed to put data in the clearing house, and that any evidence that was developed would have to be adopted and used by people in the government agencies.

Our approach was designed to build trust, leverage networks, establish value, and create a capable workforce that could do the work. We needed to build the capacity of government employees to use data to develop great ideas and inform policy. But, rather than visiting every government agency to get innovative ideas, we set up the Coleridge Initiative. This initiative established the Applied Data Analytics training program that would bring civil servants together in a research and analysis sandbox called the Administrative Data Research Facility

(ADRF). The ADRF used technology that embodied the "five safes" described in chapter 5. Of course, we worked closely with federal, state, and local staff (including George Putnam, from Illinois) to design both the ADRF and the Applied Data Analytics training program.[18]

The goal of the training program was to deliver classes that build the data skill sets for government staff to handle new types of data—by using actual data relevant to their jobs—along the lines identified by Liebman. The first set of skills focused simply on determining how to scope a problem and figure out what data are needed. We covered the entire spectrum of a project lifecycle: from problem definition and scoping to data collection, linkage, processing, analysis, and validation, as well as how to think about the ethical and privacy issues that arise when tackling these issues and communicating the results and impact effectively. We introduced new types of methods from computer science and statistics in the context of their potential to transform the scientific understanding of the dynamics of human behavior. In addition to methods, we also included an introduction to new types of data that are now available to solve problems in government agencies as well as a discussion of how to effectively incorporate them in analytical systems.

The Applied Data Analytics training program has worked. The classes have created value. They have brought people together with their colleagues from other agencies in their own and other states, and working with researchers, the civil servants identified products that would have value to their constituencies. The training programs built trust and networks with multiple state governments and state universities that have formed the basis of the partnerships necessary to create new measures and new approaches. For example, the Ohio State University offering of the Coleridge Initiative training provided government agency participants with access to integrated data from the State of Ohio on housing, education, vocational rehabilitation, unemployment insurance, and higher education combined with data from Illinois and Missouri to study the employment of people who had gone to college in Ohio, but subsequently got jobs outside of Ohio.

The value of the training and data access became excruciatingly evident in the response to the 2020 coronavirus pandemic. State agency staff who had participated in the training programs were able to work to combine multiple datasets to calculate which industries were laying off the workers claiming unemployment insurance, how many went onto the welfare rolls (including food stamps), and, based on previous shocks, where and how soon they were likely to get jobs.

In sum, the Applied Data Analytics program demonstrated the value of new ways of linking and analyzing data for solving real-world problems; promoted adoption of these practices to the benefit of the practitioners' own organizations; created a pipeline of new product prototypes central to agency missions; and generated a growing set of linked data available as an ongoing asset for use in other projects. The advantage of this approach is that it empowered public servants to identify what needed to be produced to serve their mission, while building the trust and networks across organizations among the public servants who are also the ones who know what data are best suited for what purpose.

The lessons of the LEHD program have been successful in other contexts. My experience suggests that part of the success lies in the combination of an outsider with fresh ideas, public servants committed to the shared effort, and the time to develop collaborative products to effect change. Building long-term relationships with agency staff who are permanent civil servants is a necessary, although not sufficient, condition of successfully innovating within a government agency.[19]

It is possible to empower and train the workforce so that new data can be used and new measures can be created that serve the local and regional needs of communities. As Liebman says, "If we take advantage of the great expansion in the availability of data and analysis tools to actually try to move the dial on social problems in a data-driven, outcomes-focused way, we might find that we succeed."[20]

The approach is fundamentally scalable. A data science program for public policy could be instituted in any university across the country. State and local government agencies participating in these programs through employee training and data access may enhance their ability to get access to data across jurisdictions, increase internal capacity to use these data, and develop new products that have value to their constituents. Universities participating in these programs would have an excellent way to support federal, state, and local governments, build collaborations with agencies that can support further research and education, and train students and researchers using problems and data that are locally relevant. This kind of collaboration helps state and local governments do their job of serving their constituents by using their own data, their own staff, and their own local experts while at the same time drawing on the expertise of their colleagues and experts across the nation.

In sum, this chapter has described how to build workforce capacity for working with data in government. In chapter 7, we conclude this book by examining what a new public data structure would look like.

7 THE FUTURE

How do we build a new public data infrastructure that democratizes data? How can a new system supplant the current infrastructure that—to paraphrase the president's 1995 budget—is still perforated with gaps and poorly measured, imposes too great a workload on agencies and firms, and is underutilized?[1] Put differently, how can we build an organization that will empower communities and experts to generate new data and measures that are useful to millions of users, ranging from school districts trying to figure out where to build schools, to small businesses figuring out where to locate, and to job seekers looking for work—while still producing high-quality information and protecting privacy? It's a tall order, but it's not an impossible one. All the pieces are in place in some form—they just need to be skillfully joined up.

In this chapter I describe a possible approach to establish such an infrastructure, which could be called a National Lab for Community Data (NLCD). The key elements reflect those discussed in chapters 1–6 from both LEHD and IRIS: an organizational structure that is flexible and innovative, a workforce that is skilled enough to respond to changing data needs, and a design that is responsive to local community interests. The experience of building LEHD showed us that the NLCD should be grounded in communities so that useful measures will be generated. The experience of both LEHD and IRIS was that it was necessary to integrate with universities to stay at the cutting edge of research and development while maintaining the organizational best elements that have served the public in the federal system: statistical reliability, trust, confidentiality protection, and independence. The IRIS experience showed the importance of design: that it is necessary to have flexible institutional arrangements and strong governance that ensure all participants have a voice and receive some valuable return on their investments. Decisions about governance and common goals are as important, in this view, as technical and analytic capabilities.

The previous chapters should have convinced you of the need to build such a new institution. The current federal statistical structure is hamstrung because it must continue to produce existing measures using existing approaches, and it is difficult for it to produce new measures and use new approaches. The problem will not solve itself—progress has been glacial. If insanity has been described as doing the same thing over and over and expecting a different result, perhaps the current structure should be described as doing the same thing over and over and being unable to change the result. Even when it's clear what to do, and there are many excellent staff who want to effect change, they face enormous organizational challenges in doing so.

If organizational change does not occur, public production of data will become largely extinct—because the private sector is starting to produce statistics faster and cheaper than the federal government.[2] How will government data vanish? It's already happening. Although the market forces that create change in the private sector do not exist in the public sector, legislators do feel the pressure to cut back budgets, resulting in the flatlining of statistical agency spending.[3] Citizens are also cutting their level of engagement: survey response rates are plummeting.[4] The cost of a decline in the production and use of public, trusted data would be incalculable because the resulting data are less likely to be impartial and independent, and the private sector will charge users whatever the market will bear—advantaging those businesses and individuals who can afford to pay, rather than the less wealthy users, like small businesses and low-income job seekers.

So what does organizational change entail? Chapter 5 argued that we need to rethink how to produce useful data. Chapter 6 discussed the importance of involving government workers at all levels in the creation of new data. In this chapter I argue that we need a complete rethinking of the way in which the production of data for public consumption is organized.

The work of Nobel Laureate Elinor Ostrom is extremely instructive in informing that rethinking—and is completely consistent with my experience. Her empirical study of different institutional structures led her to identify three key features of successful organizations: reputation, reciprocity, and trust. Ostrom emphasized that developing those features requires small groups, face-to-face communications, and the development of shared norms.[5] Ostrom also made it very clear that there are multiple rules that govern behavior but she could not identify specific rules that were associated with specific cases. In other words, there were no monolithic rules that all successful organizations should follow. Institutions, she argued, should simply aim at bringing out the best in each individual even while dealing with the inherent complexity of human dynamics.[6]

The current federal system is antithetical to such an approach because, as we've seen, it is too fragmented and unresponsive.

A more nimble, small-scale, small-group system is necessary to develop new measures that are valued and used—community-driven indicators. The LEHD indicators, from a program developed twenty years ago, were primitive compared with what can be done now.

The pieces necessary for this new system already exist: academic centers, programmatic agencies, and the federal statistical system. The governance structure is yet to be developed, but we have models, like IRIS, upon which to draw.

Academic centers in universities and think tanks have knowledge about and data specific to key domain areas, and they also educate students. Even in my own public policy school at NYU, faculty have collected administrative records and are building expertise in many areas, including housing (the Furman Center for Real Estate and Urban Policy), health (Health Evaluation and Analytics Lab [HEAL]), transportation (the Rudin Center for Transportation Policy and Management), and education (the Institute for Education and Social Policy). In engineering, the data that are being collected are even more high-tech—visual observation (video feeds and images), in-situ sensors, LWIR (long wavelength infrared radiation [IR]) and VNIR (visible and near IR) hyperspectral images, LiDAR (Light Detection and Ranging) topography, and satellite and other atmospheric tracking data to get high-quality data in real time.

Another example is one of the groups we've collaborated with most—Chapin Hall at the University of Chicago. It was established as an orphanage in the nineteenth century. Today it is a think tank that uses data and evidence to improve services to children, youth, and families. Chapin Hall staff, like Bob Goerge, have been recognized as pioneers in the use of human-services administrative data.[7] Their Integrated Database on Child and Family Programs in Illinois (IDB) is a unique resource for researchers and policy makers trying to understand child and family experiences in the human service, health, and education systems in Illinois.[8] IDB includes the experiences and characteristics of the entire population of Illinois children who have had contact with the child protective services, income and nutritional support, health care, education, criminal and juvenile justice, or mental health systems, in some cases dating back to the 1980s. Chapin Hall's successful working relationships with the state of Illinois, Cook County, and Chicago rest in part on the care taken to guard the confidentiality of records. In addition, they have devised ways to link the disparate data from the public agencies and paint a picture of the entire network of relationships linking children and public services—utilizing data routinely collected by the agencies for administrative purposes.[9]

Programmatic agencies—those government agencies that have to use data to administer programs—are also creating new measures in a manner that is distinct from statistical agencies. For example, at the federal level, the US Department of Health and Human Services has started the TANF (Temporary Assistance to Needy Families) Data Collaborative program, inspired by the Applied Data Analytics training program, to train state agencies that deliver welfare services on how to use data to make decisions (tanfdata.org). The TANF data collaborative is designed to accelerate the use of TANF administrative data for program improvement and evidence building at the federal, state, and local level. The US Department of Labor similarly has a program—the Workforce Information Technology Support Center—that brings together experts and data to improve decision-making. The poster child for how programmatic agencies can make successful use of data is the National Oceanic and Atmospheric Administration (NOAA), which collects about seven terabytes (TB) of data per day from hundreds of sources. Its models generate about one hundred TB of data per day and make them available[10] for such uses as weather forecasting, insurance, and resource management purposes.

Statistical agencies still have a critical role to play. They have national-level data that can be used to benchmark local indicators so that local and regional indicators can be standardized and compared. They have access to many world-class statisticians who can apply their skills to ensuring that measures are consistent over time and that the scientific integrity of new indicators developed at state and local levels meet OMB standards. Their survey expertise is still important to design measures to capture deeper understanding of economic and social behavior that the new types of data cannot measure.

There are two existing institutional models that offer inspiration for new infrastructure design. The first model is the Land Grant system established to transmit scientific expertise to members of local agricultural communities. In today's context, such an institution could be reshaped to produce interactions between governments, citizens, and universities that identify important questions, develop data, and test new useful measures.

The second institutional model to consider is the federally funded research and development center (FFRDC) system designed to provide "essential engineering, research, development, and analysis capabilities to support agencies in the performance of their responsibilities and mission."[11] The most well known of these FFRDCs are those run by the Department of

Energy—like Los Alamos National Lab, which was designed to bring experts together for the Manhattan project. This national lab model could be deployed to research and develop standards, methods, and procedures in data access, storage, documentation, management, protection, and dissemination that have a high degree of commonality across jurisdictions and centers.

The goal, therefore, is to rethink the current top-down system now in place and create a new institution—a National Lab for Community Data—that would combine the locally driven focus of the Land Grant system with a national laboratory that brings together the best talent in the country to securely store, curate, and protect social and economic data.

Advocating for a National Lab for Community Data does not mean that federal statistical agencies should be abandoned. It is not surprising, however, that their role needs to be rethought. The federal government did not grow up in the computer or internet age. Its approach to information, and data, is constrained by both the baggage that accompanies its public sector application and the burden of trying to jam a modern concept into a framework that was never designed for such change. Much is now known about how to improve the measurement of economic activity, develop new measures, and collect data very differently. But the federal government's role—so critically needed for producing high-quality statistics that the entire population can use—should be less central in identifying what data should be collected, determining how it should be collected, and performing the data collection.

Instead, we should develop a structure that plays to the strengths of the federal government. Federal agencies are the only source of consistent, long-term national frames against which the variety of different sources can be benchmarked. They have been the trusted source of statistics and can provide the long-term expertise in data governance, documentation, quality control, and confidentiality protections that are critical to good data stewardship.[12]

Many of the statistical agencies have key elements in place. For example, the USDA's Economic Research Service (ERS) partners with researchers and their sister agencies (like the Food and Nutrition Service) to use retail scanner data on product-level purchases at retail stores as well as household data to examine food policies.[13] The National Center for Education Statistics has funded statewide longitudinal data centers to better measure educational success. The Census Bureau supports state data centers, the Bureau of Justice Statistics has state analysis centers, and the National Center for Science and Engineering Statistics and the Statistics of Income Division of the IRS have active researcher partnership programs.

Creating a more functional system that will bring together the contributions of researchers, policy makers, and government agencies (in their twin roles as data producers and policy implementers) while addressing diverse interests is the operational challenge at hand. The next sections will describe the successful institutional models—and how they came to be—in more detail.

INSTITUTIONAL MODELS

How the Land Grant System Came to Be

The Land Grant system is interesting, because it is an example of a long-lived successful organizational structure—established in the nineteenth century—that ties together research, teaching, and practice. Of course, the current post-secondary system of education in the United States is now much more heterogeneous and structured very differently, but the approach taken and lessons learned could be applied to a number of institutions, regardless of whether or not they have Land Grant status.

The Land Grant system was set up in 1862, when the Morrill Land-Grant College Act provided funds to states to set aside land for colleges devoted to agriculture and the mechanical arts. The goal was to develop a system that would ensure that farmers would use modern technology to be more productive and would provide farmers with tools to implement new ideas, directly interact with research experts, and consistently innovate. If that list sounds familiar, it should—it is exactly the list of desiderata for public data in chapter 5.

In 1887, the Hatch Experiment Station Act gave states $15,000 for each of their Land Grant colleges to conduct agricultural experiments and share their research. Both basic research (work aimed purely at theory and understanding) and applied research (experiments to solve a specific problem) were to be conducted. A 1906 History of Farmers' Institutes in the United States tells the story.[14] State and local agricultural societies established farmers' institutes because farmers had a problem. Their land was beginning to show the "injurious effects of constant cropping without restoration of fertilizing elements" and they needed expert advice. Initially the farmers called meetings, and successful farmers were invited to explain their methods. Then agricultural experiment stations were formed, and scientists from those stations as well as professors from the agricultural colleges came to the meetings to give advice. These meetings were so successful that most state legislatures ended up supporting the farmers' institutes providing systematic instruction in agriculture. That approach is how new technologies and best practices were transmitted from progressive farmers and trained scientists to other farmers—and was the forerunner of the modern-day cooperative extension program.[15] The deeply local function of extension work combined with stable institutional anchors dedicated to national and even international-scale research efforts is particularly powerful: it combines the responsiveness of small-scale groups with the consistent structure of larger national organizations, avoiding the danger of collapsing into parochialism.[16]

Nowadays, the USDA (through its National Institute of Food and Agriculture) partners directly with the nation's Land Grant universities—which all retain an agricultural faculty, although the system now includes many more colleges and faculty through its cooperative extension program. The basic idea is that university faculty members translate research into practice. County-based educators work with the agricultural communities and get local input on future research priorities. Because those county educators both live and work in their communities, they build trust through long-lasting relationships and respond to local needs effectively.

The funding structure is instructive because organizations respond to financial incentives. The original Hatch Act was passed in 1887, and amended up through the Agricultural Act of 2014. There is a substantial amount of funding available to the USDA, which in 2018 spent $727 million on research and $42 million on education programs, partnering with states and others through the State Agricultural Experiment Stations (SAES). Funding for this government-supported agricultural research occurs through three mechanisms: competitive grants, capacity grants (also previously called formula grants because they were based on a standardized formula), and noncompetitive grants. It is worth examining these funding mechanisms to see if they might work for our proposed National Lab for Community Data.

If the goal is to support the generation of new ideas, *competitive grants* could be awarded to eligible post-secondary institutions for individual research (basic and applied), extension programs, and higher education activities, as well as for projects that integrate these three areas.

If the goal is to build the ability of the state and local government staff to work with data, agencies could allocate *capacity grants* to the states to enable civil servants to develop the skills to apply that research. While in the Land Grant case capacity grants are typically limited to only a certain type of institution, there is no need to be restrictive in designating which institutions of higher education should design training programs like those described in chapter 6.

Congress directs *noncompetitive grants* to support designated institutions for research, education, or extension programs on topics of particular importance to a state or region. Imagine Congress designating some centers to specialize in producing new indicators on opioid addiction, income mobility, or whatever pressing societal problem is of current interest—just as the University of Wisconsin specializes in research on apple production and the University of Texas on cattle production. In other words, the structure could be put in place to establish regional and local data centers with a skilled workforce that can quickly respond to local or regional needs.

How the FFRDC System Came to Be

The Land Grant system works well as a coordination mechanism between farmers and researchers. But because of privacy and technology challenges, the statistical data problems need more infrastructure. This is where the model of national labs comes into play.

Created at the onset of the Cold War, federally funded research and development centers were designed to make available to the government the unique resources and capabilities assembled during World War II, such as MIT's Radiation Laboratory and the assets of the Manhattan Project.[17] Since then, the FFRDC mechanism has evolved beyond its origins in national security. With twelve federal agencies now sponsoring a total of forty-two FFRDCs, these organizations are intended to provide their sponsors with stable workforces composed of highly trained technical talent that have the ability to address long-term, extremely complex problems with a high degree of objectivity.

FFRDCs fall into three broad categories, all of which could be helpful in developing an ecosystem for developing and securely sharing data in forms that can be integrated into a national platform: (1) R&D laboratories, (2) study and analysis centers, and (3) system engineering and integration centers.[18] Their missions encompass areas as diverse as national, homeland, and nuclear security; aviation and space; health; fundamental science; climate research; and federal agency modernization.

R&D laboratories include labs that are large, highly-specialized scientific and engineering facilities exploring a range of topics for their agency sponsors, from particle accelerators and x-ray light sources for the Department of Energy (DOE), to ground-based telescopes for NSF, to facilities that produce pharmaceuticals used in NIH clinical trials while applying good manufacturing practices.

Some of these FFRDCs also develop research capabilities at the scale necessary to address major, long-term challenges. For example, R&D FFRDCs have been used to develop essential, closely held expertise in cryptology and cybersecurity for the intelligence community. Not all R&D lab FFRDCs are national labs—only DOE R&D laboratory FFRDCs have that title. The DOE's Office of Science operates well-known labs like Oakridge and Fermi, while the National Nuclear Security Administration operates others like Sandia National Lab and Los Alamos.

Study and analysis centers deliver independent and objective analyses and advise in core areas important to their sponsors in support of policy development, decision-making, alternative approaches, and new ideas on issues of significance to the sponsor's mission. Agencies sponsoring study and analysis FFRDCs include the Army, Navy, Centers for Medicare and Medicaid Services (CMS), Department of Homeland Security (DHS), the Nuclear Regulatory Commission, and NSF. As an example, CMS established the Alliance to Modernize Healthcare (the "Health FFRDC") in 2012 to combine large-scale-enterprise system engineering with specialized health-subject-matter expertise in order to transform delivery of the nation's healthcare services.

System engineering and integration centers often play a critical role in assisting their sponsors in technically formulating, initiating, and evaluating programs that are eventually procured from firms in the for-profit sector. These FFRDCs may create or help the sponsor choose system concepts and architectures. They may specify technical system, subsystem, and interface requirements while supporting the sponsor in the development and acquisition of system hardware and software, the testing and verification of performance, and the integration of new capabilities. Sponsors look to these system engineering FFRDCs for approaches that offer continuous improvement of system and logistical operations. Agencies sponsoring systems engineering FFRDCs include the Administrative Office of the United States Courts, the Air Force, the Internal Revenue Service, National Institute of Standards and Technology (NIST), the Social Security Administration, the Under Secretary of Defense for Research and Engineering, and the Veterans Administration. For example, the Judiciary Engineering and Modernization Center sponsored by the Administrative Office of the US Courts is investigating whether automated legal analysis could be used to rapidly resolve simple cases that are transactionally complex because they straddle multiple administrative layers, such as cases involving building codes or regulatory proceedings. If successful, this could be one strategy to alleviate clogged court dockets and reduce backlogs at administrative agencies.

Because FFRDCs are intended to have access to the federal government, its data, and specialized equipment, and because that access can exceed what's provided by normal contractual relationships, a higher bar is set for establishing and reviewing FFRDCs. Among the requirements, agencies must demonstrate the inability of existing sources to meet the specialized research or development needs; they must publish notices of intent to establish an FFRDC in the Federal Register and notify the Office of Science and Technology Policy; and they must be able to provide reasonable continuity in the level of support for the FFRDC. In exchange, the FFRDC, which must be operated by an autonomous organization or an identifiably separate unit of a parent organization, is required to operate in the public interest, be free from organizational conflicts of interest, and fully disclose its affairs to the primary sponsor.[19]

The funding model is different from that of the Land Grant system. FFRDCs have a sponsoring agency that provides long-term funding: the resultant continuity and stability enable it to hire and retain top talent. Although there is both congressional and executive branch oversight, the system has been criticized for the lack of competition, and there is an increasing push to make funding more competitive so FFRDCs don't have a perpetual, unmerited existence. The system is not perfect—there are concerns about the effectiveness of federal agency oversight and management of FFRDCs; inappropriate competition between FFRDCs and the private sector for federal R&D funding; the diversification of FFDRC activities or "mission creep"; and the award of noncompetitive FFRDC management and operation contracts.[20]

However, there is some external discipline. Since the first FFRDC was established in 1947, more than sixty-two FFRDCs have closed, merged, split, or been delisted as FFRDCs—some so they could compete openly. The US Department of Health, Education, and Welfare—a predecessor of today's Department of Education—closed more than thirty of its FFRDCs in the early 1970s. Several FFRDCs migrated to different contractual mechanisms, such as Johns Hopkins University's Applied Physics Laboratory, which became a University Affiliated Research Center to better integrate the university's education and research missions. Recompetition for the contracts to operate FFRDCs is increasingly common. Beginning in the George W. Bush administration, the DOE recompeted a number of its management and operations contracts previously held exclusively by universities and effectively required them to partner with industrial concerns as a means of bolstering the project management and operational rigor of those national labs.[21]

A NATIONAL LAB FOR COMMUNITY DATA

The establishment of a National Lab for Community Data could bring the best elements of both of these two institutional models together. We will need an organizational structure that is national in scale while connecting to local communities, just like the Land Grant system model. The structure will need to be focused on building cutting-edge R&D in response to complex problems. And there will need to be funding vehicles so that federal, state, and local agencies can support that R&D.

Accordingly, one way of thinking about the design of a National Lab for Community Data would be to take the pieces of the national lab system as a model for R&D and funding, and the model of Land Grant universities for training, coordination, and outreach. The infrastructure would provide the data so that evidence can be built in an open, transparent, and democratic way. The NLCD could be set up as a networked organization, with centers throughout the country participating in the network.

Access to protected data could be designed with privacy and confidentiality controls that are baked in from the start. The NLCD would provide state-of-the-art technical strategies and thoughtful human oversight and screening to dramatically improve privacy and usage protections. A variety of standardized mechanisms have already been developed for different confidentiality situations, ranging from de-identification, to mathematical mechanisms to add noise to data, to secure enclaves (ultimately in the cloud) with mechanisms for certifying safe users, safe analyses, and safe products. These mechanisms should be extended and improved continually. Legal hurdles, often created in the name of confidentiality when current protection methods did not exist, can be addressed while increasing security by developing more up-to-date templates that could be widely used. Most importantly, the NLCD's governance would be structured to ensure stakeholder input, possibly modeled after the successful hub-and-node governance structure employed by IRIS.

Some base of stable funding is critical. The technology for data sharing is expensive to build and maintain, and high-quality staff are difficult to hire and retain. Take, for example, building a cloud-based computing environment so that confidential microdata can be hosted and shared. The Federal Risk and Authorization Management Program (FedRAMP) is a government-wide program that takes a standardized approach to security. But it costs several million dollars to establish a FedRAMP-certified facility, and hundreds of thousands of dollars a year to comply with all the rules necessary to ensure complete isolation of, and controlled access to, data. High-quality staff are necessary to build tools that can serve many local needs at scale. For example, if multiple agencies want to allow multiple users to have access to multiple projects with different rules, start dates, and end dates, it is critical to have reliable and automated data stewardship tools. Agencies also need to be allowed and enabled to monitor the use of sensitive data across federal, state, and local governments. Building collaborative tools so that code can be shared and teams can work on joint projects to ensure reproducibility of analysis requires top staff and system continuity. Likewise, as discussed in earlier chapters, systems must be developed and put in place to develop feedback loops for the search and discovery of analytical datasets so that researchers know which datasets are being used, for which research subjects, with what tools, as well as the methods used and findings from the research. All the infrastructure work, while foundational, is an investment that needs an ongoing source of stable funding. We are faced with very hard technical challenges that do not have a silver bullet and that will need computer scientists, domain scientists, and government analysts to work together for many years to continually address problems.

That stable funding could come from a sponsoring agency, just as the national lab system is funded by the Department of Energy. The sponsoring agency would need to demonstrate that an NLCD would meet federal requirements that "existing alternative sources for satisfying agency requirements cannot effectively meet the special research or development needs." The case made in this book is that an NLCD should be structured to meet federal tests of carrying out "work that is critical to maintaining control of an agency's mission and operations" and respond to the Federal Data Strategy's call for "a robust, integrated approach to using data to deliver on mission, serve customers, and steward resources while respecting privacy and confidentiality."[22]

Governance is critical if the vision of democratizing data is to be achieved. The NLCD could have three foci, representing the three stakeholder groups that would make up the organization.

The first focus would be local in nature—ensuring it has democratic community roots. It would support state and local government agencies in identifying questions of key interest to local communities. As I have pointed out throughout the book, agencies already have strong connections with their constituencies and well-established professional associations and the NLCD could build on those connections. It would feature a distributed university-based data and education program in the cooperative extension style in the development and use of data designed to respond to those questions. It would be designed to bring together university centers and local government agencies. As noted, many government agencies already have state programs in all fifty states, and most universities have bureaus of economic research and often specialized centers in such areas as housing, workforce, criminal justice, and education policy. Almost every major university has now established centers for data science—schools of public policy, education, or criminal justice could partner with those centers and with their statistics departments, combining their domain expertise to provide new sources of trained human capital to both the city agencies and the private sector. Academic researchers, again acting in partnership with the data science community, could be brought in to inform future data collection as well as new ways to process, store, analyze, and disseminate data.

The second focus would be on ensuring national comparability, longitudinal consistency, and quality. This necessitates building a mechanism to set national standards and establish a secure environment so that state and local governments, and other stakeholders, could have an efficient, secure way of combining and comparing their data. This mechanism could be the role of the federal government, except not confined as it currently is to statistical agencies but expanded to include programmatic agencies like the Departments of Labor and Health and Human Services. The programmatic agencies could be tasked to support the development of common standards among the states in the administration of their government programs. The statistical agencies could be tasked to establish benchmarks for cross-state comparisons as well as statistical quality standards so that the public would know what measures to trust. The basic foundation has already been put into place by the Foundations for Evidence-Based Policymaking Act of 2018, as noted earlier in the book, which requires that agencies appoint chief data officers, evaluation officers, and statistical officials, and establish data governance bodies.

The third focus would be ensuring that innovation is baked in. There needs to be a mechanism whereby the NLCD is rewarded for developing new ideas, creating new data, and promulgating new measures. As such, the business model of the organization must be designed to have grant and contract funding as part of the revenue stream. Historically, philanthropic foundations and industry funding have often been in the vanguard of supporting new ideas; in the case of the National Lab for Community Data, industry might also provide new forms of data as well.

We need a serious, coordinated investment strategy to protect confidentiality in order to reduce access barriers, and to build state and local capacity to use data in order to produce valuable new information.[23] Then, for example, state and local agencies could use their own data to let students, parents, and teachers know what are successful education pathways, and doctors would be able to make use of accurate local housing data to predict whether children are at risk of lead poisoning.[24] Training programs would empower government agency staff, business owners, and students with the knowledge and expertise essential to create new measures that matter to them. New tools would enable data owners to test innovations and figure out what is working and what is not.

This vision is achievable. Commitment is necessary to design and build such a new approach. We have existing successes to guide us. We can use these successes to develop a coordinated national investment strategy, and authorize an institutional structure that can support the wise use of data. It is the responsibility of our government to use data to ensure that the Joe Salvos of this country can get the data they need for emergency management, that small businesses and workers get information about jobs and earnings, and that the children in all counties, not just Allegheny County, are safer. And even more urgently, that information about the economic and social impact of massive sudden shocks like the coronavirus pandemic can be gathered and provided to decision makers quickly and accurately.

That would fulfill the promise of a democratized public data infrastructure.

Notes

CHAPTER 1

1. E. Brynjolfsson and A. McAfee, "The Big Data Boom Is the Innovation Story of Our Time," *Atlantic*, November 21, 2011, https://www.theatlantic.com/business/archive/2011/11/the-big-data-boom-is-the-innovation-story-of-our-time/248215/.

2. J. Norwood, *Organizing to Count: Change in the Federal Statistical System* (Washington, DC: Urban Institute Press, 1995).

3. Norwood, *Organizing to Count*; C. F. Citro, "The US Federal Statistical System's Past, Present, and Future," *Annual Review of Statistics and Its Application* 3 (2016): 347–373; J. E. Triplett, "The Federal Statistical System's Response to Emerging Data Needs," *Journal of Economic and Social Measurement* 17 (1991): 155–177.

4. J. Auerbach et al., "Will Administrative Data Save Government Surveys?" *Significance* 16 (2019): 35–39.

5. G. West, "Defunding Statistical Agencies Poses Risks to Economies and Public Knowledge," *Sunlight Foundation*, May 24, 2017, https://sunlightfoundation.com/2017/05/24/defunding-statistical-agencies-poses-risks-to-economies-and-public-knowledge/; American Statistical Association (ASA), "Other Leaders Maintain USDA's Upheaval of Research Arm Unwise, Counterproductive," *Eureka Alert*, March 12, 2019, https://www.eurekalert.org/pub_releases/2019-03/asa-aol031219.php.

6. B. Appelbaum, *The Economists' Hour: False Prophets, Free Markets, and the Fracture of Society* (New York: Little, Brown and Company, 2019).

7. S. Winchester, *The Perfectionists: How Precision Engineers Created the Modern World* (New York: HarperCollins Publishers, 2018), 331.

8. National Research Council, *Modernizing the U.S. Census* (Washington, DC: National Academies Press, 1994).

9. Government Accountability Office (GAO), *High Risk Report: 2020 Census* (Washington, DC: GAO, 2017).

10. M. Cynamon, "National Health Interview Survey Questionnaire Redesign," National Center for Health Statistics (2016), http://www.copafs.org/User Files/file/NHISRedesignforCOPAFSrev.pdf.

11. US Department of Commerce, United States Census Bureau, *US Census Bureau's Budget: Fiscal Year 2020* (March 2019), https://www2.census.gov/ about/budget/FY-2020-Congressional-Budget-Submission.pdf.

12. Since the cost to each household is that it takes about 40 minutes to answer and the average US hourly wage is $27.

13. See United States Census Bureau, "American Community Survey (ACS)," https://www.census.gov/programs-surveys/acs.

14. "Local Laws of the City of New York for the Year 2009," http://legistar.council .nyc.gov/View.ashx?M=F&ID=4550139&GUID=2D8B50C9-5E56-486F -AB53-5701172A1084.

15. "Local Laws of the City of New York for the Year 2016," http://legistar.council .nyc.gov/View.ashx?M=F&ID=899223&GUID=263FF0C1-D8A6-4669 -B25F-5A25B33FBFF4.

16. The Council of the City of New York, *Committee Report of the Human Services Division, Committee on Education*, November 22, 2016, http://legistar.council .nyc.gov/View.ashx?M=F&ID=4802163&GUID=42D379F0-C48A-47C8 -90D9-40F1D418F295

17. S. E. Spielman, D. Folch, and N. Nagle, "Patterns and Causes of Uncertainty in the American Community Survey," *Applied Geography* 46 (2014): 147– 157.

18. F. Navarro, "An Introduction to ACS Statistical Methods and Lessons Learned," presented at Measuring People in Place conference, October 5, 2012, Boulder, CO.

19. A. Beveridge, "Can Differentially Privatized Data Be Used for Redistricting?," presented at Association of Public Data Users conference, July 9, 2019, Arlington, VA.

20. M. Hansen, "To Reduce Privacy Risks, the Census Plans to Report Less Accurate Data," *New York Times*, December 5, 2018, https://www.nytimes.com/2018/12/05/upshot/to-reduce-privacy-risks-the-census-plans-to-report-less-accurate-data.html.

21. S. E. Spielman and A. Singleton, "Studying Neighborhoods Using Uncertain Data from the American Community Survey: A Contextual Approach," *Annals of the American Association of Geographers* 105 (2015): 1003–1025.

22. Ibid.

23. Ibid.

24. S. Galloway, *The Four: The Hidden DNA of Amazon, Apple, Facebook, and Google* (New York: Portfolio/Penguin, 2017).

25. E. Wagner, "OPM Announces New 'Data Scientist' Job Title," *Government Executive*, July 1, 2019, https://www.govexec.com/management/2019/07/opm-announces-new-data-scientist-job-title/158139/.

26. H. E. Brady, "The Challenge of Big Data and Data Science," *Annual Review of Political Science* 22 (2019): 297–323.

27. D. Donoho, "50 Years of Data Science," *Journal of Computational and Graphical Statistics* 26, no. 4 (2017): 745–766, https://doi.org/10.1080/10618600.2017.1384734.

28. Editorial Board, "Our Privacy Regime Is Broken. Congress Needs to Create New Norms for a Digital Age," *Washington Post*, January 5, 2019, https://www.washingtonpost.com/opinions/our-privacy-regime-is-broken-congress-needs-to-create-new-norms-for-a-digital-age/2019/01/04/c70b228c-0f9d-11e9-8938-5898adc28fa2_story.html?utm_term=.8b4114001456.

29. US Census Bureau, North American Industry Classification System, 2017 NAICS, https://www.census.gov/cgi-bin/sssd/naics/naicsrch?chart=2017.

30. Galloway, *The Four*.

31. Ibid.

32. Ibid.

33. R. M. Groves, "Three Eras of Survey Research," *Public Opinion Quarterly* 75 (2011): 861–871.

34. Norwood, *Organizing to Count.*

CHAPTER 2

1. P. Aldrick, "Review of *The Growth Delusion: The Wealth and Wellbeing of Nations* by David Pilling," *Times Saturday Review* (2018): 14–15.

2. Robert F. Kennedy, Remarks at the University of Kansas, March 18, 1968.

3. A. Brandolini and E. Viviano, "Measuring Employment and Unemployment," *IZA World Labor* (2018): doi:10.15185/izawol.445.

4. C. Hokayem, C. Bollinger, and J. P. Ziliak, "The Role of CPS Nonresponse in the Measurement of Poverty," *Journal of the American Statistical Association* 110 (2015): 935–945; K. G. Abraham, J. Haltiwanger, K. Sandusky, and J. R. Spletzer, "Exploring Differences in Employment between Household and Establishment Data," *Journal of Labor Economics* 31 (2013): S129–S172.

5. K. G. Abraham, J. Haltiwanger, K. Sandusky, and J. R. Spletzer, "Exploring Differences in Employment between Household and Establishment Data."

6. D. Philipsen, *The Little Big Number: How GDP Came to Rule the World and What to Do About It* (Princeton: Princeton University Press, 2015).

7. J. S. Landefeld, E. P. Seskin, and B. M. Fraumeni, "Taking the Pulse of the Economy: Measuring GDP," *Journal of Economic Perspectives* 22 (2008): 193–216.

8. B. M. Fraumeni, "Gross Domestic Product: Are Other Measures Needed?," *IZA World Labor* (2017), https://wol.iza.org/articles/gross-domestic-product-are-other-measures-needed/long, accessed January 31, 2020.

9. D. Coyle, *GDP: A Brief but Affectionate History* (Princeton: Princeton University Press, 2015).

10. G. Ehrlich, J. C. Haltiwanger, R. S. Jarmin, D. Johnson, and M. D. Shapiro, *Big Data for 21st Century Economic Statistics* (Chicago: University of Chicago Press, 2019).

11. Brandolini and Viviano, "Measuring Employment and Unemployment."

12. Ibid.

13. The Economist, "Plunging Response Rates to Household Surveys Worry Policymakers," *Economist*, May 24, 2018, https://www.economist.com/inter national/2018/05/24/plunging-response-rates-to-household-surveys-worry -policymakers.

14. S. Finer, *The History of Government from the Earliest Times. Volume III: Empires, Monarchies and the Modern State* (Oxford: Oxford University Press, 1997).

15. D. Pilling, *The Growth Delusion: The Wealth and Well-Being of Nations* (New York: Bloomsbury Press, 2018).

16. Coyle, *GDP*; Finer, *History of Government from the Earliest Times,* vols. 1–3.

17. Coyle, *GDP*.

18. Ibid.

19. Although the Englishman Alfred Marshall's 1890 book (*Principles of Economics*) foreshadowed many of the ideas.

20. Ehrlich et al., *Big Data for 21st Century Economic Statistics*; The Economist, "Plunging Response Rates to Household Surveys Worry Policymakers."

21. Philipsen, *Little Big Number*.

22. Coyle, *GDP*.

23. R. W. Fogel et al., "The Emergence of National Income Accounting as a Tool of Economic Policy," in *Political Arithmetic: Simon Kuznets and the Empirical Tradition in Economics*, ed. Robert William Fogel, Enid M. Fogel, Mark Guglielmo, and Nathaniel Grotte (Chicago: University of Chicago Press, 2013), 49–64.

24. Philipsen, *Little Big Number*.

25. Ibid.

26. Coyle, *GDP*.

27. Landefeld, Seskin, and Fraumeni, "Taking the Pulse of the Economy."

28. C. S. Carson, "The History of the United States National Income and Product Accounts: The Development of an Analytical Tool," *Review of Income and Wealth* 21 (1975): 153–181.

29. Landefeld, Seskin, and Fraumeni, "Taking the Pulse of the Economy."

30. Pilling, *Growth Delusion*; David Pilling, *The Growth Delusion: Wealth, Poverty, and the Well-Being of Nations* (New York: Tim Duggan Books, 2018); Fogel et al., "Emergence of National Income Accounting."

31. Ehrlich et al., *Big Data for 21st Century Economic Statistics*; J. Norwood, *Organizing to Count: Change in the Federal Statistical System* (Washington, DC: The Urban Institute Press, 1995).

32. Ehrlich et al., *Big Data for 21st Century Economic Statistics*.

33. Coyle, *GDP*.

34. M. Feldstein, "Underestimating the Real Growth of GDP, Personal Income, and Productivity," *Journal of Economic Perspectives* 31 (2017): 145–164.

35. Philipsen, *Little Big Number*; D. Coyle, *The Political Economy of National Statistics* (Oxford: Oxford University Press, 2016).

36. E. Brynjolfsson and A. Saunders, "What the GDP Gets Wrong (Why Managers Should Care)," *MIT Sloan Management Review* 51 (2009): 95.

37. J. Lane, "Uses of Microdata: Keynote Speech," in *Statistical Confidentiality and Access to Microdata* (Geneva, Switzerland: UNECE, 2003), https://www.unece.org/fileadmin/DAM/stats/publications/statistical.confidentiality.pdf.

38. The Economist, "The Hounding of Greece's Former Statistics Chief Is Disturbing," *Economist*, June 14, 2018.

39. Norwood, *Organizing to Count*.

40. Coyle, *GDP*; Ehrlich et al., *Big Data for 21st Century Economic Statistics*; D. W. Jorgenson, J. S. Landefeld, and P. Schreyer, *Measuring Economic Sustainability and Progress* (Chicago: University of Chicago Press, 2014), http://www.nber.org/books/jorg12-1; E. Brynjolfsson, A. Collis, and F. Eggers, "Using Massive Online Choice Experiments to Measure Changes in Well-Being," *Proceedings of the National Academy of Science* 116 (2019): 7250–7255; C. Corrado, C. Hulten, and D. Sichel, "Intangible Capital and US Economic Growth," *Review of Income and Wealth* 55 (2009): 661–685; J. Haskel and S. Westlake, *Capitalism Without Capital: The Rise of the Intangible Economy* (Princeton: Princeton University Press, 2017).

41. Brian Moyer and Abe Dunn, "Measuring the Gross Domestic Product (GDP): The Ultimate Data Science Project," Harvard Data Science Review, January 31, 2020, https://hdsr.mitpress.mit.edu/pub/5pkkan15.

42. Office of Information and Regulatory Affairs, OMB, *Questions and Answers When Designing Surveys for Information Collections* (2016), https://obamawhitehouse.archives.gov/sites/default/files/omb/inforeg/pmc_survey_guidance_2006.pdf.

43. R. M. Groves, "Three Eras of Survey Research," *Public Opinion Quarterly* 75 (2011): 861–871; R. M. Groves and L. Lyberg, "Total Survey Error: Past, Present, and Future," *Public Opinion Quarterly* 74 (2010): 849–879; F. Kreuter, "Data Collection and Inference," keynote speech at the European Survey Research Association, July 14, 2015, Reykjavik, Iceland.

44. US Census Bureau, "History of the Current Population Survey (CPS)," (2015), https://www.census.gov/programs-surveys/cps/about/history-of-the-cps.html; US Bureau of Labor Statistics and US Census Bureau, "History of the Current Population Survey," chapter 2, https://www2.census.gov/programs-surveys/cps/methodology/Techincal paper 66 chapter 2 history.pdf; Norwood, *Organizing to Count.*

45. US Bureau of Labor Statistics, "Labor Force Statistics from the Current Population Survey" (2015), https://www.bls.gov/cps/cps_htgm.htm - concepts, accessed August 22, 2019.

46. Brandolini and Viviano, "Measuring Employment and Unemployment."

47. Groves and Lyberg, "Total Survey Error."

48. US Census Bureau, *Basic CPS Items Booklet: Labor Force Items*, https://www2.census.gov/programs-surveys/cps/techdocs/questionnaires/Labor%20Force.pdf?#.

49. Fogel et al., "Emergence of National Income Accounting."

50. K. C. Jones, "No Handheld Devices for 2010 Census," *InformationWeek*, April 3, 2008, https://www.informationweek.com/mobile/no-handheld-devices-for-2010-census-/d/d-id/1066429.

51. J. A. Yates and D. S. Rothstein, "The Newest National Longitudinal Survey: The National Longitudinal Survey of Youth 1997," *Industrial Relations: A Journal of Economy and Society* 38 (1999): 604–610; M. R. Pergamit, C. R. Pierret, D. S. Rothstein, and J. R. Veum, "The National Longitudinal Surveys," *Journal of Economic Perspectives* 15 (2001): 239–253.

52. W. Moore et al., *National Longitudinal Survey of Youth 1997 (NLSY97): Technical Sampling Report* (Chicago: National Opinion Research Center, 2000), https://www.bls.gov/nls/nlsy97techsamp.pdf, accessed January 31, 2020.

53. R. J. A. Little and D. B. Rubin, *Statistical Analysis with Missing Data, 3rd ed.* (New York: John Wiley & Sons, 2019).

54. OMB, "Standards and Guidelines for Statistical Surveys," US Office of Management and Budget (Sept. 2006).

55. J. Lane, V. Stodden, S. Bender, and H. Nissenbaum, eds., *Privacy, Big Data, and the Public Good: Frameworks for Engagement* (Cambridge: Cambridge University Press, 2014); P. Doyle, J. Lane, J. Theeuwes, and L. Zayatz, eds., *Confidentiality, Disclosure and Data Access: Theory and Practical Applications for Statistical Agencies* (Amsterdam: North-Holland, 2001).

56. K. McGeeney et al., *2020 Census Barriers, Attitudes and Motivators Study Survey Report,* US Census Bureau, Washington, DC (2019).

57. D. Lind and L. Nelson, "The Fight over the 2020 Citizenship Question, Explained," *Vox*, June 12, 2019, https://www.vox.com/policy-and-politics/2019/6/12/18663009/census-citizenship-question-congress.

58. M. Anderson and W. Seltzer, "The Dark Side of Numbers: The Role of Population Data Systems in Human Rights Abuses," *Social Research 68* (2001): 481–513.

59. S. Ruggles, C. Fitch, D. Magnuson, and Jonathan Schroeder, "Differential Privacy and Census Data: Implications for Social and Economic Research," *AEA Papers & Proceedings* 109 (2019): 403–408.

60. N. F. Potok, "Creating Useful Integrated Data Sets to Inform Public Policy," dissertation, The George Washington University, 2009.

61. Fogel et al., "Emergence of National Income Accounting."

62. A. Bennett, *Forty Years On and Other Plays* (London: Faber, 1991).

63. Jennifer Cohen Kabaker, "Guidance on ARRA Reporting Requirements from OMB," July 6, 2019, https://www.newamerica.org/education-policy/federal-education-budget-project/ed-money-watch/guidance-on-arra-reporting-requirements-from-omb/.

64. Norwood, *Organizing to Count.*

CHAPTER 3

1. Cited in J. Norwood, *Organizing to Count, Change in the Federal Statistical System* (Washington, DC: The Urban Institute Press, 1995).

2. E. Lichtblau, "Profiling Report Leads to a Clash and a Demotion," *New York Times*, August 24, 2005, https://www.nytimes.com/2005/08/24/us/front page/41asq.html.

3. American Statistical Association Board Statement to Greek officials, May 17, 2018, https://www.amstat.org/ASA/News/ASA-Board-Decries-Second-Annul ment-of-Former-Greece-Chief-Statisticians-Acquittal.aspx, retrieved February 3, 2020.

4. See https://www.whitehouse.gov/wp-content/uploads/2018/06/Government -Reform-and-Reorg-Plan.pdf.

5. "26 U.S. Code § 6103.Confidentiality and Disclosure of Returns and Return Information," Legal Information Institute, https://www.law.cornell.edu/uscode/ text/26/6103.

6. Norwood, *Organizing to Count*.

7. National Research Council, *Improving Business Statistics Through Interagency Data Sharing: Summary of a Workshop* (Washington, DC: National Academies Press, 2006).

8. K. Fairman, L. Foster, C. J. Krizan, and I. Rucker, "An Analysis of Key Differences in Micro Data: Results from the Business List Comparison Project," *US Census Bureau Center for Economic Studies Paper No. CES-WP-08–28* (2008).

9. G. Ehrlich, J. C. Haltiwanger, R. S. Jarmin, D. Johnson, and M. D. Shapiro, "Reengineering National Statistics," in *Big Data for 21st Century Economic Statistics*, ed. Katharine G. Abraham, Ron S. Jarmin, Brian Moyer, and Matthew D. Shapiro (Chicago: University of Chicago Press, forthcoming).

10. Ibid.

11. Norwood, *Organizing to Count*.

12. M. Hurwitz and J. Smith, "Student Responsiveness to Earnings Data in the College Scorecard," *Economic Inquiry* 56 (2018): 1220–1243.

13. N. Ghaffarzadegan, R. Larson, and J. Hawley, "Education as a Complex System," *Systems Research and Behavioral Science* 34 (2017): 211.

14. M. Davern, "Data User Perspectives on Potential Changes to Data Products to Protect Privacy," presented at Challenges and New Approaches for Protecting Privacy in Federal Statistical Programs workshop, Committee on National Statistics, June 7, 2019, Washington DC, http://sites.nationalacad emies.org/cs/groups/dbassesite/documents/webpage/dbasse_193521.pdf, accessed January 31, 2020

15. S. Ruggles, "Implications of Differential Privacy for Census Bureau Data and Scientific Research," (2018), working paper 2018-6, Minnesota Population Center, University of Minnesota.

16. "Researchers Question Census Bureau's New Approach to Privacy," September 28, 2019, https://wtop.com/national/2019/09/researchers-question-census -bureaus-new-approach-to-privacy/.

17. E. L. Groshen, "Importance of the US Bureau of Labor Statistics and Critical Issues It Faces," *Business Economics* 53 (2018): 86–99.

18. Commission on Evidence-Based Policymaking, *The Promise of Evidence-Based Policymaking: Report of the Commission on Evidence-Based Policy* (2017), http://www.cep.gov/; The National Academies of Sciences, Engineering, and Medicine, *Federal Statistics, Multiple Data Sources, and Privacy Protection: Next Steps* (Washington, DC: The National Academies Press, 2017), https://www.nap.edu/catalog/24893/federal-statistics-multiple-data-sources -and-privacy-protection-next-steps.

19. UNECE, "Sustainable Development Goals," https://www.unece.org/stats/ documents/2019.06.ces.html.

20. M. Kanellos, "152,000 Smart Devices Every Minute in 2025: IDC Outlines the Future of Smart Things," *Forbes* March 3, 2016, https://www.forbes.com/ sites/michaelkanellos/2016/03/03/152000-smart-devices-every-minute-in -2025-idc-outlines-the-future-of-smart-things/#611b0d04b63e.

21. H. Schank and S. Hudson, "Hawaii's False Alert Shows the Sorry State of Government Technology," *Washington Post*, January 19, 2018.

22. M. Weber, "The Essentials of Bureaucratic Organization: An Ideal-Type Construction," *Reader in Bureaucracy* 19 (1952): 19–21.

23. D. P. Carpenter, *The Forging of Bureaucratic Autonomy: Reputations, Networks, and Policy Innovation in Executive Agencies, 1862–1928* (Princeton: Princeton University Press, 2001).

24. National Research Council, *Principles and Practices for a Federal Statistical Agency*, 5th ed., ed. C. F. Citro and M. L. Straf (Washington, DC: The National Academies Press, 2013).

25. Ibid.

26. V. Nirala, "Janet Norwood (1923–2015): A Pioneer and an Inspiration," *Amstat News* (blog), December 8, 2016, https://magazine.amstat.org/blog/2016/12/08/sih-norwood/.

27. Norwood, *Organizing to Count.*

28. Defined as programs that spent $500,000 annually on statistical activities.

29. National Research Council, *Principles and Practices for a Federal Statistical Agency.*

30. The White House, President Barack Obama, "The Structure of the Federal Statistical System," https://obamawhitehouse.archives.gov/omb/inforeg_stat policy/bb-structure-federal-statistical-system.

31. The Confidential Information Protection and Statistical Efficiency Act, title 3 of Pub.L. 115-435.

32. National Research Council, *Principles and Practices for a Federal Statistical Agency.*

33. National Institute of Standards and Technology, "Interagency Committee on Standards Policy (ICSP)," https://www.nist.gov/standardsgov/what-we-do/federal-policy-standards/interagency-committee-standards-policy-icsp, accessed January 31, 2020.

34. National Research Council, *Principles and Practices for a Federal Statistical Agency.*

35. J. T. Bonnen, "Federal Statistical Coordination Today: A Disaster or a Disgrace?" *The American Statistician* 37 (1983): 179–192.

36. Sylvia Morrison, *Federal Economic Statistics: Would Closer Coordination Make for Better Numbers?* (92–784E), Congressional Research Service, 1992. As quoted in GAO, *Statistical Agencies Adherence to Guidelines and Coordination of Budgets*, 65th ed., vol. 95 (Washington, DC: United States General Accounting Office, 1995).

37. GAO, *Statistical Agencies Adherence to Guidelines and Coordination of Budgets.*

38. C. Benson, "The Data Catch: Not Enough Information," *CQ Weekly, December 7, 2009, 2810.*

39. Ibid.

40. K. McGeeney et al., *2020 Census Barriers, Attitudes and Motivators Study Survey Report* (Washington, DC: US Census Bureau, 2019).

41. M. Anderson et al., "Sampling-Based Adjustment of the 2000 Census—a Balanced Perspective," Jurimetrics (2000): 341–356.

42. M. Holland and J. I. Lane, "Policy Advisory Committees: An Operational View," *Policy Analysis in the United States*, ed. J. Hird (Bristol University Press, 2018), 173–182.

43. Ibid.

44. Ibid.

45. S. L. Moffitt, "Promoting Agency Reputation through Public Advice: Advisory Committee Use in the FDA," *Journal of Politics* 72 (2010): 880–893.

46. C. Corrado, C. Hulten, and D. Sichel, in *Measuring Capital in the New Economy* (Chicao: University of Chicago Press, 2005), 11–46; C. Corrado, C. Hulten, and D. Sichel, "Intangible Capital and US Economic Growth," *Review of Income and Wealth* 55 (2009): 661–685.

47. Holland and Lane, "Policy Advisory Committees."

48. US Census Bureau, "Federal Statistical Research Data Centers," https://www.census.gov/fsrdc.

49. D. Card, R. Chetty, M. Feldstein, and E. Saez, "Expanding Access to Administrative Data for Research in the United States" (2011), http://emlab.berkeley.edu/~saez/card-chetty-feldstein-saezNSF10dataaccess.pdf.

50. J. Lane, "Big Data for Public Policy: The Quadruple Helix," *Journal of Policy Analysis and Management* 35, no. 3 (2016): 708–715.

51. D. S. Evans, R. Schmalensee, and S. Murray, "The Census Bureau Needs to Significantly Revise Reporting and Calculation of Its Online and Physical Retail Sales Figures and Commission an Independent Review," February 8, 2016, http://dx.doi.org/10.2139/ssrn.2728918.

52. There are, of course, other institutions that have deep knowledge on how to collect and disseminate data. Some are well-known survey research organizations like Pew, Gallup, Westat, RTI, and NORC, which have their own

field organizations and indeed are often used as data collectors by the agencies themselves. There are innumerable professional organizations as well, such as the American Association for Public Opinion Research for survey methodologists, the Population Association of America for demographers, and the National Association of Business Economists. Many private sector companies also repackage and process statistical data information for smaller organizations.

53. United Nations Statistical Commission, "Fundamental Principles of Official Statistics Endorsed by the General Assembly as Resolution A/RES/68/261" (New York, 2014), available at https://unstats.un.org/unsd/dnss/gp/FP-New-E.pdf, accessed January 31, 2020.

54. Commission on Evidence-Based Policymaking, *The Promise of Evidence-Based Policymaking: Report of the Commission on Evidence-Based Policy* (2017), http://www.cep.gov/.

55. 115th United States Congress, Foundations for Evidence-Based Policymaking Act of 2018 (2018).

CHAPTER 4

1. A. H. Teich, "In Search of Evidence-Based Science Policy: From the Endless Frontier to SciSIP," *Annals of Science and Technology Policy* (2018), doi:10.1561/110.00000007.

2. D. Antenucci, M. Cafarella, M. Levenstein, C. Ré, and M. D. Shapiro, "Using Social Media to Measure Labor Market Flows," NBER Working Paper No. 20010 (National Bureau of Economic Research, 2014).

3. "Prediction of Initial Claims for Unemployment Insurance," University of Michigan Economic Indicators from Social Media, latest estimate July 15, 2017, http://econprediction.eecs.umich.edu/.

4. L. Japec et al., "Big Data in Survey Research AAPOR Task Force Report," *Public Opinion Quarterly* 79 (2015): 839–880.

5. D. R. Olson, K. J. Konty, M. Paladini, C. Viboud, and L. Simonsen, "Reassessing Google Flu Trends Data for Detection of Seasonal and Pandemic Influenza: A Comparative Epidemiological Study at Three Geographic Scales," *PLoS Computational Biology* 9 (2013): e1003256; H. Choi and H. Varian, "Predicting the Present with Google Trends," *Economic Record* 88 (2012): 2–9; S. Cook, C. Conrad, A. L. Fowlkes, and M. H. Mohebbi,

"Assessing Google Flu Trends Performance in the United States during the 2009 Influenza Virus A (H1N1) Pandemic," *PLoS ONE* 6 (2011): e23610.

6. D. Lazer, R. Kennedy, G. King, and A. Vespignani, "The Parable of Google Flu: Traps in Big Data Analysis," *Science* 343 (2014): 1203–1205.

7. J. K. Hakes and R. D. Sauer, "An Economic Evaluation of the Moneyball Hypothesis," *Journal of Economic Perspectives* 20 (2006): 173–186.

8. E. Brynjolfsson, L. Hitt, and H. Kim, "Strength in Numbers: How Does Data-Driven Decisionmaking Affect Firm Performance?" (2011): SSRN 1819486.

9. P. M. Romer, "The Deep Structure of Economic Growth," February 5, 2019, https://paulromer.net/deep_structure_growth/.

10. J. Lane, "Let's Make Science Metrics More Scientific," *Nature* 464 (2010): 488–489.

11. N. Zolas et al., "Wrapping It Up in a Person: Examining Employment and Earnings Outcomes for PhD Recipients," *Science* 360 (2015): 1367–1371.

12. J. Lane, "Let's Make Science Metrics More Scientific"; J. Lane and S. Bertuzzi, "Measuring the Results of Science Investments," *Science* 331 (2010): 678–680; B. Bozeman and E. Corley, "Scientists' Collaboration Strategies: Implications for Scientific and Technical Human Capital," *Research Policy* 33 (2004): 599–616; P. E. Stephan, *How Economics Shapes Science* (Cambridge, MA: Harvard University Press, 2012).

13. Zolas et al., "Wrapping It Up in a Person"; J. I. Lane, N. Goldschlag, B. A. Weinberg, and N. Zolas, "Proximity and Economic Activity: An Analysis of Vendor-Business Transactions," *Journal of Regulatory Science 59, no. 1* (2019): 67–83.

14. W.-Y. Chang, W. Cheng, J. Lane, and B. Weinberg, "Federal Funding of Doctoral Recipients: What Can Be Learned from Linked Data," *Research Policy* 48 (2019): 1487–1492.

15. J. Marburger, "Wanted: Better Benchmarks," *Science* 308 (2005): 1087.

16. J. Gitlin, "Calculating the Economic Impact of the Human Genome Project," National Human Genome Research Institute, posted May 2011, last updated June 12, 2013, https://www.genome.gov/27544383/calculating-the-economic-impact-of-the-human-genome-project.

17. National Academy of Sciences, *Data on Federal Research and Development Investments: A Pathway to Modernization* (Washington, DC: National Resources Council, 2010).

18. K. Husbands Fealing, J. I. Lane, J. L. King, and S. Johnson, *Measuring the Economic Impact of Research: The Case of Food Safety* (Cambridge, Cambridge University Press, 2018).

19. K. B. Whittington, J. Owen-Smith, and W. W. Powell, "Networks, Propinquity, and Innovation in Knowledge-Intensive Industries," *Administrative Science Quarterly* 54 (2009): 90–122; W. Powell and E. Giannella, "Collective Invention and Inventor Networks," in *The Handbook of Innovation*, ed. Bronwyn Hall and Nathan Rosenberg (Amsterdam: Elsevier, 2010), 575–605.

20. Important work has been done by Adam Jaffe (A. B. Jaffe, "Real Effects of Academic Research," *American Economic Review* (1989): 957–970); Audretsch and Feldman (D. B. Audretsch and M. P. Feldman, "Innovative Clusters and the Industry Life Cycle," *Review of Industrial Organization* 11 (1996): 253–273; and D. B. Audretsch and M. P. Feldman, "R&D Spillovers and the Geography of Innovation and Production," *American Economic Review* (1996): 630–640), Audretsch and Stephan (D. B. Audretsch and P. E. Stephan, "Company-scientist Locational Links: The Case of Biotechnology," *American Economic Review* (1996): 641–652) among others using the existing data.

21. Work by Paula Stephan and coauthors are important exceptions; E. J. Reedy, M. Teitelbaum, and R. E. Litan, "The Current State of Data on the Science and Engineering Workforce, Entrepreneurship, and Innovation in the United States," in *The Handbook of Science Policy*, ed. K. H. Fealing, J. Lane, J. H. Marburger, and S. Shipp (Stanford: Stanford University Press, 2011), 208–231.

22. National Institutes of Health, *Biomedical Research Workforce Working Group Report* (2012).

23. Sally Rockey, "Taking on the Challenge of Better Biomedical Workforce Data," *Rock Talk*, April 11, 2013, http://nexus.od.nih.gov/all/2013/04/11/taking-on-the-challenge-of-better-biomedical-workforce-data/.

24. Reedy, Teitelbaum, and Litan, "Current State of Data"; National Institutes of Health, *Draft Report of the Advisory Committee to the Director Working Group on Diversity in the Biomedical Research Workforce* (2012).

25. D. Walsh, "Not Safe for Funding: The N.S.F. and the Economics of Science," *New Yorker*, May 6, 2013, http://www.newyorker.com/online/blogs/elements/2013/05/peer-review-politics-economics-of-science.html.

26. D. Lipinski, in *Opening Statement on the Science of Science and Innovation Policy, Hearing before the Subcommittee on Research and Science Education, Committee on Science and Technology House of Representatives, 111th Congress, Second Session,* Sebtember 23, 2010, https://www.govinfo.gov/content/pkg/CHRG-111hhrg58486/html/CHRG-111hhrg58486.htm.

27. M. Florio, *Investing in Science: Social Cost-Benefit Analysis of Research Infrastructures* (Cambridge, MA: MIT Press, 2019).

28. P. Azoulay, "Research Efficiency: Turn the Scientific Method on Ourselves," *Nature* 484 (2012): 31–32.

29. European Commission, "The 3% Objective—a Brief History" (2008), http://ec.europa.eu/invest-in-research/action/history_en.htm.

30. Hakes and Sauer, "An Economic Evaluation of the Moneyball Hypothesis."

31. European Research Council, "ERC Frontier Research Leaves Its Mark: 73% Breakthroughs or Major Advances," 11-09-2017, https://erc.europa.eu/news/2017-qualitative-evaluation-projects.

32. Romer, "The Deep Structure of Economic Growth."

33. Unfortunately, by that time Jack Marburger had died, but not before we had coedited a book, *The Handbook of Science Policy* (Stanford: Stanford University Press, 2011), which laid out the vision that lies at the foundation of IRIS.

34. J. I. Lane, J. Owen-Smith, R. F. Rosen, and B. A. Weinberg, "New Linked Data on Research Investments: Scientific Workforce, Productivity, and Public Value," *Research Policy* (2015), doi:10.1016/j.respol.2014.12.013.

35. A. Ikudo, J. Lane, J. Staudt, and B. A. Weinberg, "Occupational Classifications: A Machine Learning Approach," *Journal of Economic and Social Measurement* (2020): preprint 1–31.

36. Zolas et al., "Wrapping It Up in a Person"; N. Goldschlag et al., "Research Funding and Regional Economies," *NBER Working Paper* 23018 (2017).

37. National Research Council, *Furthering America's Research Enterprise* (Washington, DC: The National Academies Press, 2014); Office of Science and Technology Policy, *The Science of Science Policy: A Federal Research Roadmap*

(2008), https://apps.dtic.mil/dtic/tr/fulltext/u2/a496840.pdf, accessed January 31, 2020.

38. A. H. Teich, "In Search of Evidence-Based Science Policy: From the Endless Frontier to SciSIP," *Annals of Science and Technology Policy* (2018), doi:10.1561/110.00000007.

39. National Academies of Science, Engineering, and Medicine, *Graduate STEM Education for the 21st Century*, ed. A. Leshner and L. Scherer (Washington, DC: The National Academies Press, 2018); E. Cady and P. P. Reid, "Understanding the Educational and Career Pathways of Engineers," *American Society for Engineering Education* (2018), doi:10.17226/XXXXX.09-26-18; National Academies of Science, Engineering, and Medicine, *Measuring the 21st Century Science and Engineering Workforce Population: Evolving Needs* (Washington, DC: The National Academies Press, 2018); National Academies of Science, Engineering, and Medicine, *Envisioning the Data Science Discipline: The Undergraduate Perspective—Interim Report* (Washington, DC: The National Academies Press, 2018); National Academies of Science, Engineering, and Medicine, *Promising Practices for Strengthening the Regional STEM Workforce Development Ecosystem* (Washington, DC: The National Academies Press, 2016); American Academy of Arts & Sciences, *Public Research Universities: Recommitting to Lincoln's Vision—an Educational Compact for the 21st Century* (Cambridge, MA: American Academy of Arts & Sciences, 2016); Commission on Evidence-Based Policymaking, *The Promise of Evidence-Based Policymaking: Report of the Commission on Evidence-Based Policy* (2017), http://www.cep.gov/; National Academies of Science, Engineering, and Medicine, *Enhancing the Effectiveness of Team Science*, ed. N. J. Cooke and M. L. Hilton (Washington, DC: The National Academies Press, 2015); and National Academies of Science, Engineering, and Medicine, *Returns to Federal Investments in the Innovation System: Proceedings of a Workshop—in Brief* (Washington, DC: The National Academies Press, 2017), doi:10.17226/24905.

CHAPTER 5

1. Joseph Salvo, "2020 Census Data Products: The Data Users' Perspective," June 7, 2019, Population Division, NYC Planning, http://sites.nationalacad emies.org/cs/groups/dbassesite/documents/webpage/dbasse_193520.pdf.

2. P. Doyle, J. Lane, J. Theeuwes, and L. Zayatz, eds., *Confidentiality, Disclosure and Data Access: Theory and Practical Applications for Statistical Agencies* (Amsterdam: North-Holland, 2001).

3. S. J. Barbeau, A. Borning, and K. Watkins, "OneBusAway Multi-region— Rapidly Expanding Mobile Transit Apps to New Cities," *Journal of Public Transportation* 17 (2014): 3; C. A. Le Dantec, K. E. Watkins, R. Clark, and E. Mynatt, "Cycle Atlanta and OneBusAway: Driving Innovation through the Data Ecosystems of Civic Computing," in *Human–Computer Interaction Users and Context, Proceedings 17th International Conference, HCI International 2015, Part III*, ed. M. Kurosu (Amsterdam: Springer, 2015), 327–338.

4. H. Kim, C. Wildeman, M. Jonson-Reid, and B. Drake, "Lifetime Prevalence of Investigating Child Maltreatment among US Children," *American Journal of Public Health* 107 (2017): 274–280; A. Chouldechova, D. Benavides-Prado, O. Fialko, and R. Vaithianathan, "A Case Study of Algorithm-Assisted Decision Making in Child Maltreatment Hotline Screening Decisions," in *Proceedings of the 1st Conference on Fairness, Accountability and Transparency, PMLR 81* (2018): 134–148.

5. L. MacFarquhar, "When Should a Child Be Taken from His Parents?," *New Yorker*, July 31, 2017.

6. R. Thebault, "Parents Reported Their 5-Year-Old Son Missing. Now They're Charged with Murder," *Washington Post*, April 25, 2019, https://www.washingtonpost.com/crime-law/2019/04/24/parents-reported-their-year-old -son-missing-now-theyre-charged-with-murder/?utm_term=.cc3cd468e816.

7. D. Hurley, "Can an Algorithm Tell When Kids Are in Danger?" *New York Times Magazine*, January 2, 2018, https://www.nytimes.com/2018/01/02/ magazine/can-an-algorithm-tell-when-kids-are-in-danger.html.

8. J. D. Goldhaber-Fiebert and L. Prince, "Impact Evaluation of a Predictive Risk Modeling Tool for Allegheny County's Child Welfare Office" (2019), https://www.alleghenycountyanalytics.us/wp-content/uploads/2019/05/ Impact-Evaluation-from-16-ACDHS-26_PredictiveRisk_Package_050119 _FINAL-6.pdf.

9. D. Warsh, "A Few Words about the Vladimir Chavrid Award," *Economic Principals*, December 13, 2010.

10. S. Burgess, J. Lane, and J. Theeuwes, "The Uses of Longitudinal Matched Employer/Employee Data in Labor Market Analysis," in *Proceedings of the American Statistical Association* (1998).

11. J. Haltiwanger, J. Lane, J. Spletzer, and J. Theeuwes, "International Symposium on Linked Employer-Employee Data," *Monthly Labor Review* 121 (1998): 48; J. C. Haltiwanger, J. I. Lane, J. R. Spletzer, J. Theeuwes, and K. Troske, eds., *The Creation and Analysis of Employer-Employee Matched Data* (Amsterdam: North-Holland, 1999).

12. S. Burgess, J. Lane, and D. Stevens, "Job Flows, Worker Flows, and Churning," *Journal of Labor Economics* 18, no. 3 (2000): 473–502.

13. A. Golan, J. Lane, and E. McEntarfer, "The Dynamics of Worker Reallocation Within and Across Industries," *Economica* 74 (2017): 1–20.

14. D. Warsh, "Paradigms, after 50 Years," *Economic Principals*, December 23, 2012, http://www.economicprincipals.com/issues/2012.12.23/1449.html.

15. J. Abowd, J. Haltiwanger, and J. Lane, "Integrated Longitudinal Employee-Employer Data for the United States," *American Economic Review* 94 (2014): 224–229.

16. J. Lane, Uses of Microdata: Keynote Speech," in *Statistical Confidentiality and Access to Microdata* (Geneva, Switzerland: UNECE, 2003), https://www.unece.org/fileadmin/DAM/stats/publications/statistical.confidentiality.pdf.

17. J. Lane, "Big Data for Public Policy: The Quadruple Helix," *Journal of Policy Analysis and Management* 35, no. 3 (2016): 708–715.

18. Topos, "Promoting Data Sharing Approaches" (forthcoming), https://www.topospartnership.com/about-us/.

19. L. Sweeney, "Computational Disclosure Control: A Primer on Data Privacy Protection," Ph.D. diss., Massachusetts Institute of Technology, Cambridge (2001).

20. M. Barbaro, T. Zeller, and S. Hansell, "A Face Is Exposed for AOL Searcher No. 4417749," *New York Times*, August 9, 2016.

21. K. Hill, "How Target Figured Out a Teen Girl Was Pregnant before Her Father Did," *Forbes,* February 16, 2012.

22. S. K. Kinney and A. Karr, "Public-Use vs. Restricted-Use: An Analysis Using the American Community Survey," *U.S. Census Bureau Center for Economic*

Studies Discussion Paper No. CES-WP-17–12 (2017); other approaches, like licensing, have become less popular because of the difficulty of tracking use and providing updates.

23. See https://www.ukdataservice.ac.uk/manage-data/legal-ethical/access-control/ five-safes.

24. L. Beringer, A. Petcher, Q. Y. Katherine, and A. W. Appel, "Verified Correctness and Security of OpenSSL {HMAC}," in *24th {USENIX} Security Symposium ({USENIX} Security 15)* (2015), 207–221. https://www.usenix.org/ system/files/conference/usenixsecurity15/sec15-paper-beringer.pdf, accessed January 31, 2018.

25. C. Landwehr, "Engineered Controls for Dealing with Big Data," in *Privacy, Big Data, and the Public Good: Frameworks for Engagement*, ed. J. Lane, V. Stodden, S. Bender, and H. Nissenbaum (Cambridge: Cambridge University Press, 2014) 211–233; S. Bender and J. Heining, "The Research-Data-Centre in Research-Data-Centre Approach: A First Step towards Decentralised International Data Sharing," *IASSIST Quarterly* 35 (2011): 10–16.

26. C. Dwork, "Differential Privacy: A Cryptographic Approach to Private Data Analysis," in *Privacy, Big Data, and the Public Good: Frameworks for Engagement*, ed. J. Lane, V. Stodden, S. Bender, and H. Nissenbaum (Cambridge: Cambridge University Press, 2014), 296–322.

27. L. Wissler et al., "The Gold Standard in Corpus Annotation," in *IEEE GSC* 22 (2014), https://pdfs.semanticscholar.org/124f/69e9549535f07bc77f29ff 91b8330aa429a0.pdf, accessed January 31, 2020.

28. N. Zolas et al., "Wrapping It Up in a Person: Examining Employment and Earnings Outcomes for Ph.D. Recipients," *Science* 350 (2015): doi:10.1126/ science.aac5949.

29. M. Vardigan, P. Heus, and W. Thomas, "Data Documentation Initiative: Toward a Standard for the Social Sciences," *International Journal of Digital Curation* 3 (2008): 107–213.

30. Giwon Hong et al., "Finding Datasets in Publications: The KAIST Approach," in *Where's Waldo*, ed. J. Lane, Paco Nathan, and I. Mulvany (SAGE Publications, forthcoming), http://34.82.145.119:8080/.

31. C. Xiong, R. Power, and J. Callan, "Explicit Semantic Ranking for Academic Search via Knowledge Graph Embedding," in *Proceedings of the 26th Interna-*

tional Conference on World Wide Web (International World Wide Web Conferences Steering Committee, 2017), 1271–1279.

32. Topos, "Promoting Data Sharing Approaches," 9.

33. Topos, "Promoting Data Sharing Approaches."

CHAPTER 6

1. R. M. Goerge, "Engagement with State and Local Government," SocArXiv, June 12, 2019, https://osf.io/preprints/socarxiv/v6tc2/; A. Reamer et al., eds., "Developing the Basis for Secure and Accessible Data for High Impact Program Management, Policy Development, and Scholarship," *Annals of the American Academy of Political and Social Science* 675, no. 1 (2018), https://journals.sagepub.com/toc/anna/675/1; A. Reamer and J. Lane, "A Roadmap to a Nationwide Data Infrastructure for Evidence-Based Policymaking," *Annals of the American Academy of Political and Social Science* 675, no. 1 (2018): 28–35, https://doi.org/10.1177/0002716217740116.

2. Goerge, "Engagement with State and Local Government."

3. J. B. Liebman, "Using Data to More Rapidly Address Difficult U.S. Social Problems," *Annals of the American Academy of Political and Social Science* 675 (1) (2017): 166–181, https://journals.sagepub.com/doi/full/10.1177/0002716217745812.

4. Ibid.

5. Goerge, *Handbook.*

6. S. Bender and J. Tokle, "Record Linkage," in *Big Data Meets Social Science,* ed. I. Foster, R. Ghani, R. Jarmin, F. Kreuter, and J. I. Lane (London: Taylor & Francis, 2016), 71–92.

7. T. C. Fort and S. D. Klimek, *The Effects of Industry Classification Changes on US Employment Composition,* Working Paper, Tuck at Dartmouth (2016).

8. W. E. Winkler, *Methods for Record Linkage and Bayesian Networks,* Technical Report (Washington, DC: Statistical Research Division, US Census Bureau, 2002).

9. D. Warsh, "A Few Words about the Vladimir Chavrid Award," *Economic Principals,* December 13, 2010.

10. S. Burgess, J. Lane, and J. Theeuwes, "The Uses of Longitudinal Matched Employer/Employee Data in Labor Market Analysis," in *Proceedings of the American Statistical Association* (Arlington, VA: American Statistical Association, 1998).

11. J. C. Haltiwanger, J. I. Lane, J. R. Spletzer, J. Theeuwes, and K. Troske, eds., *The Creation and Analysis of Employer and Employee Matched Data* (Amsterdam: North-Holland, 1999).

12. G. Peters and D. J. Savoie, *Governance in the Twenty-First Century: Revitalizing the Public Service* (Quebec, CA: McGill-Queen's Press-MQUP, 2000).

13. N. Zolas, N. Goldschlag, R. Jarmin, P. Stephan, J. Owen-Smith, and R. F. Rosen et al., "Wrapping It Up in a Person: Examining Employment and Earnings Outcomes for Ph.D. Recipients," *Science* 350 (2015): 6266.

14. Warsh, "A Few Words about the Vladimir Chavrid Award."

15. Commission on Evidence-Based Policymaking, *The Promise of Evidence-Based Policymaking* (Washington, DC: CEP 2017), www.cep.gov.

16. Ibid., 1.

17. J. Mays, "Building an Infrastructure for Evidence-Based Policymaking: A View from a State Administrator," *Annals of the American Academy of Political and Social Science Ann. Am. Acad. Pol. Soc. Sci.* 675 (1) (Dec. 21 2017): 41–43, https://doi.org/10.1177/0002716217739275.

18. I. Foster et al., *Big Data and Social Science: A Practical Guide to Methods and Tools* (London: Taylor & Francis Group, 2016); F. Kreuter, R. Ghani, and J. I. Lane, "Change through Data: A Public Extension Program for Government Employees," *Harvard Data Science Review* 1, no. 1 (2019), https://doi.org/10.1162/99608f92.ed353ae3.

19. Goerge, "Engagement with State and Local Government."

20. Liebman, "Using Data to More Rapidly Address Difficult U.S. Social Problems."

CHAPTER 7

1. J. Norwood, *Organizing to Count, Change in the Federal Statistical System.* (New York: Urban Institute, 1995).

2. A. Oyedele, "The 2 Most Popular Ways to Track the US Jobs Market Are Telling Wildly Different Stories," *Business Insider*, July 6, 2017, https://

markets.businessinsider.com/news/stocks/us-jobs-report-adp-bls-gap-2017
-7-1002152177.

3. Office of Management and Budget, *Using Administrative and Survey Data to Build Evidence* (Washington, DC: OMB, 2016), https://www.whitehouse .gov/sites/default/files/omb/mgmt-gpra/using_administrative_and_survey _data_to_build_evidence_0.pdf.

4. National Academies of Sciences, Engineering, and Medicine, *Innovations in Federal Statistics: Combining Data Sources while Protecting Privacy* (Washington, DC: The National Academies Press, 2017).

5. J. Lane, "Building an Infrastructure to Support the Use of Government Administrative Data for Program Performance and Social Science Research," *Annals of the American Academy of Political and Social Science* 675, no. 1 (2018): 240–252.

6. E. Ostrom, "Beyond Markets and States: Polycentric Governance of Complex Economic Systems," *Transnational Corporate Review* 2, no. 2 (2010): 1–12.

7. H. Allen, I. Garfinkel, and J. Waldfogel, "Social Policy Research in Social Work in the Twenty-First Century: The State of Scholarship and the Profession; What Is Promising, and What Needs to Be Done," *Social Service Review* 92, no. 4 (2018): 504–547.

8. R. Goerge, J. Van Voorhis, and B. J. Lee, "Illinois's Longitudinal and Relational Child and Family Research Database," *Social Science Computer Review* 23, no. 4 (1994): 351–365.

9. R. M. Goerge, "Engagement with State and Local Government," SocArXiv, June 12, 2019, https://osf.io/preprints/socarxiv/v6tc2/.

10. Joshua New, "Five Q's for Ed Kearns, Chief Data Officer at NOAA," Center for Data Innovation, April 21, 2017, https://www.datainnovation.org/ 2017/04/5-qs-for-ed-kearns-chief-data-officer-at-noaa/.

11. Office of Management and Budget, Office of Federal Procurement Policy (OFPP), *Policy Letter 11–01, Performance of Inherently Governmental and Critical Functions* (F.R. 56227, September 12, 2011), 76.

12. National Academies of Science, Engineering, and Medicine, *Proposed Revisions to the Common Rule for the Protection of Human Subjects in the Behavioral and Social Sciences* (Washington, DC: The National Academies Press, 2014).

13. M. K. Muth, M. Sweitzer, D. Brown, K. Capogrossi, S. A. Karns, and D. Levin et al., *Understanding IRI Household-Based and Store-Based Scanner Data* (Washington, DC: USDA ERS, 2016).

14. J. Hamilton, "History of Farmers' Institutes in the United States," *United States Department of Agriculture, Office of Experimental Stations, Bulletin* no. 174 (1906).

15. J. Alston and P. Pardey, *Making Science Pay* (Washington, DC: American Enterprise Institute, 1996).

16. J. Owen-Smith, *Research Universities and the Public Good: Discovery for an Uncertain Future* (Stanford: Stanford University Press, 2018).

17. MITRE, *FFRDCs—a Primer: Federally Funded Research and Development Centers in the 21st Century* (McLean, VA: MITRE, 2015), https://www.mitre.org/sites/default/files/publications/ffrdc-primer-april-2015.pdf.

18. National Science Foundation, National Center for Science and Engineering Statistics, *Master Government List of Federally Funded R&D Centers* (Alexandria, VA: NSF 2019).

19. Federal Acquisition Regulation 48 CFR § 35.017–2: *Establishing or Changing an FFRDC*.

20. Ibid.

21. National Science Foundation, *Master Government List of Federally Funded R&D Centers*; Office of Management and Budget. *Federal Data Strategy* (Washington, DC, 2019), https://strategy.data.gov/; R. M. Goerge, "Barriers to Accessing State Data and Approaches to Addressing Them," *Annals of the American Academy of Political and Social Science* 675 (1) (Dec. 21, 2017): 122–137, https://doi.org/10.1177/0002716217741257.

22. Office of Management and Budget, *Federal Data Strategy* (Washington, DC: OMB, 2019), https://strategy.data.gov.

23. J. Lane, "Big Data for Public Policy: The Quadruple Helix," *Journal of Policy Analysis and Management* 35, no. 3 (2016): 708–715.

24. Nurfilzah Rohaidi, "This Scientist Used Analytics to Fight Child Lead Poisoning," *Energy Insider*, n.d., https://govinsider.asia/smart-gov/rayid-ghani-data-science-public-policy-lead-poisoning/.

Index

Abowd, John, 90–91
Academic centers, 124–125
Academic community, 58–59, 122
Administrative data, 88, 91, 111,
     117–118
Administrative Data Research Facility
     (ADRF), 117–118
Advisory committees, 56–57
Agricultural Act of 2014, 130
Agricultural research, 129–131
Agriculture, US Department of, 52,
     130
Allegheny County Office of Children,
     Youth and Families (CYF), 86–87,
     107
Alliance to Modernize Healthcare,
     133
Amazon, 101
American Community Survey (ACS),
     6–9, 83–84
American Recovery and Reinvestment
     Act, 39
Anderson, Margo, 36
Applied Data Analytics training pro-
     gram, 117–119
Automated legal analysis, 134

Bennett, Allan, 38
Benson, Clea, 53
Berndt, Ernie, 31
Bretton Woods conference, 26
Brin, Sergey, 73
Brynjolfsson, Erik, 29, 31
Bureau of Economic Analysis, 44
Bureau of Justice Statistics, 128
Bureau of Labor Statistics, 38, 43–44
Business registers, 43–44

Capacity grants, 131
Card, David, 59
Carter, Jimmy, 51
Categories, consistency of, 112
Census Bureau, US, 5, 128
     American Community Survey
          (ACS), 6–9, 83–84
     business register, 43–44
     confidentiality, 45
     and congressional oversight, 54–55
     Current Population Survey (CPS),
          20, 31–34
     Decennial Census, 34, 36, 54–55
     and employer-employee data, 90–91,
          111

Census Bureau (cont.)
  funding, 53
  and IRIS, 66, 76–77, 80
  and LEHD program, 108, 112–113
  and privacy, 7–8
  sampling, 54–55
  spending data, 44
Centers for Disease Control and
  Prevention, 69
Centers for Medicare and Medicaid
  Services (CMS), 133
Chapin Hall, 124–125
Chetty, Raj, 59
Chief data officers (CDOs), 13
Chief statistician, 49–50
Child poverty, 8
Children, Youth and Families (CYF),
  Allegheny County Office of, 86–
  87, 107
Child services system, 86–87, 92
Clark, Colin, 37
Classification consistency, 112
Clinton administration, 41–42
Cloud computing, 95
Coleridge Initiative, 117–119
Commission on Evidence-Based Poli-
  cymaking, 57, 61, 116–117
Committee for Institutional Coopera-
  tion (CIC), 76
Committee on National Statistics, 58
Competitive grants, 131
Conference for Research on Income
  and Wealth (CRIW), 58
Confidentiality, 45, 60, 85, 140. See
  also Privacy
  and employer-employee data, 88–89
  federal agency protections, 91–92

and reidentification, 93, 95–96
Congressional committees, 53
Construct validity, 32
Corrado, Carol, 31
Council of Professional Associations
  on Federal Statistics, 58
Coyle, Diane, 30
Current Population Survey (CPS), 20,
  31–34

Data. See also Datasets; Public data;
  Value of data
  collection, 127
  combining, 111–112
  de-identification of, 95
  duplication of, 43–44
  linked, 79–80
  new, 46–47, 63–64
  personalized, 83
  skills, 13–14, 118
  transaction, 78–79
Data Documentation Initiative (DDI),
  99
Data Revolution, 2
Datasets, 98–102
  consistency of classification, 112
  ontology, 99
  recommender engine, 101
  registry, 100
  semantic context, 100–101
  tagging, 98
  user engagement, 101–102
data.world, 101
Decennial Census, 54–55
  of 2010, 34
  of 2020, 36
De-identification of data, 95

Department of Defense, 69–70, 73
Department of Energy (DOE), 133
Disambiguation problem, 111
Duplication of data, 43–44

Economic Research Service (ERS), 128
Education measures, 44–45
Employer-employee data, 88–91, 111
Employment outcomes, 80
Employment statistics, 20–23
Entity resolution problem, 111
European Research Council (ERC), 74
Evans, David, 59
Extension program, agricultural, 130

Facebook, 10
Farmers' institutes, 129–130
Federal Data Strategy, 13, 61, 103, 138
Federal Funds Survey, 68–69
Federally funded research and development center (FFRDC) system, 126–127, 132–136
Federal Register, 33
Federal Statistical Research Data Centers, 58, 77
Federal statistical system, 3. *See also* Public data; Surveys
  and academic community, 58–59
  and advisory committees, 56–57
  budgeting, 52–57
  and congressional committees, 53
  coordination of, 49–52
  current data, 84
  and data collection, 127
  data skills, 13–14, 118
  features of, 6

fragmentation of, 42–43, 123–124
  and Great Recession of 2008, 39
  insiders and outsiders, 107–108, 110–114
  key characteristics of, 60
  multiple agencies of, 48–49
  and new data, 46–47
  privacy protections, 91–92
  and private sector, 10–11, 85, 122–123
  reliability of data, 6–9
  restructuring, 12–13
  salaries, 109
  structure of, 16
  technological and human resources, 47
  trust in, 60
  and value of data, 115
Federal Support Survey, 69–70
FedRAMP, 95, 137
Feldstein, Martin, 28, 59
Fellowships, 114
"Five safes" framework, 93–96, 104–105
Florio, Massimo, 73
Flu incidence, 64
Forty Years On, 38
Foundations for Evidence-Based Policymaking Act of 2018, 13, 61, 103, 140
Funding
  agricultural research, 130–131
  categories of, 69–70
  and congressional committees, 53
  and economic activity, 65–66, 72
  fellowships, 114
  FFRDCs, 135–136

Funding (cont.)
    grants, 131
    and labor inputs, 71–72
    and measurement, 21, 67–75
    NLCD, 137–138
    public data, 3
    R&D, 68–70
    results of, 72–73

GDP: A Brief but Affectionate History,
    30
General Motors, 10
George, Bob, 124
Georgiou, Andreas, 42
GitHub, 102
Google, 64, 73
Gordon, Nancy, 91, 112
Govern for America, 114
Government. *See* Federal statistical
    system
Government Accountability Office
    (GAO), 56
Grants, 131
Great Depression, 24–26
Great Recession of 2008, 39
Greece, 42
Gross domestic product (GDP), 14,
    19–31
    calculating, 27
    consequences of, 27–28
    and Great Depression, 26
    limitations of, 29–30
    and political influence, 30
    and price adjustments, 28–29
    real GDP, 28–29
    reliability of, 19–22, 29–30
    and retail sales, 59

and World War II, 26
Gross national product (GNP), 26
Groves, Bob, 35
Growth Delusion, The, 23

Haltiwanger, John, 90
Harrah's Casinos, 64
Hatch Experiment Station Act, 129–
    130
Health FFRDC, 133
HMAC (Hashed Message Authentica-
    tion Code), 96
Households
    list of, 7
    sampling, 55
Human Genome Project, 67–68, 73

Income, national, 25, 28
Infant mortality, 109–110
Information, 11, 15
Innovation, 38, 140. *See also* Institute
    for Research on Innovation and
    Science (IRIS)
Insiders and outsiders, industry, 107–
    108, 110–114
Institute for Research on Innovation
    and Science (IRIS), 63–68, 121–
    122
    and Census Bureau, US, 66, 76–77,
    80
    development of, 65–67, 75–76, 81
    measurement challenge, 67–68
    multiple data sources, 79–80
    organizational nodes, 77
    and research universities, 80
    transactions, 78–79
    UMETRICS, 63, 66–67, 76–78, 98

Integrated Database on Child and Family Programs in Illinois (IDB), 125
Interagency Council on Statistical Policy (ICSP), 50

Jackson, Henry, 108, 113, 115
Japanese internment, 36
Job data, 88–90
Job outcomes, 44–45
Jobs numbers, 20
Job-to-Job Flows, 90
Judiciary Engineering and Modernization Center, 134

Kennedy, Robert F., 19, 30
Keynes, John Maynard, 24
Knowledge bases, developing, 98–102
Knowledge graphs, 101–102
Kuznets, Simon, 25, 28, 37, 57

Land Grant system, 126, 128–131
Liberty Island example, 7–8
Liebman, Jeff, 109–110, 116, 118, 120
Linked data, 79–80
Little Big Number, The, 21
Longitudinal Employer-Household Dynamics (LEHD) program, 88–91, 115–116
and Census Bureau, 108, 112–113
and NLCD, 121–122
Los Alamos National Lab, 127
Lyberg, Lars, 35

Marburger, Jack, 68, 73, 75
McFadden Allen, Barbara, 76

Measurement, 14–15
and anecdotal data, 74
of economic activity, 25
and funding, 21, 67–75
GDP, 27–29
of research impact, 67–75
self-evaluation, 74
Military taxation, 23–24
"Moneyball," 64
Morrill Land-Grant College Act, 129
Moyer, Brian, 31
Murray, Patty, 116
Murray, Scott, 59

NASA, 70
National Academies of Sciences, Engineering, and Medicine, 56, 58
National Bureau of Economic Research (NBER), 25, 37, 58
National Center for Education Statistics, 128
National Center of Science and Engineering Statistics (NCSES), 66, 68, 128
National Health Interview Survey, 5
National income measurement, 25, 28
National Institute of Food and Agriculture, 130
National Institutes of Health (NIH), 70–73
National Lab for Community Data (NLCD), 127, 136–141
funding, 137–138
governance, 138–140
and LEHD program, 121–122
National Longitudinal Survey of Youth 1997, 34–35

National Oceanic and Atmospheric Administration (NOAA), 85, 126
National Science Foundation (NSF), 70, 73
National Secure Data Service, 61
National Weather Service, 85
Necker, Jacques, 24
New data, 46–47, 63–64
Noncompetitive grants, 131
Norwood, Janet, 2, 17, 30, 43, 49, 52
NYU, 124

Office of Information and Regulatory Affairs (OIRA), 49–51
Office of Management and Budget (OMB), 41, 49–52
On-the-job training, 88–89
On-The-Map, 89–90
Ontology, dataset, 99
Oppenheimer, Robert, 66, 113
Organizations
  change in, 123
  key features of success, 123
Organizing to Count: Change in the Federal Statistical System, 49
Ostrom, Elinor, 123
Owen-Smith, Jason, 68, 76–77

Page, Larry, 73
Petty, William, 24
Philipsen, Dirk, 21
Pilling, David, 23
Post Secondary Employment Outcomes, 90
Potok, Nancy, 37
Poverty, child, 8
Presidential election of 2016, 20

Price adjustments, 28–29
Privacy. *See also* Confidentiality
  child services system, 86–87
  "five safes" framework, 93–96, 104–105
  privacy/utility tradeoff, 92
  and reliability of data, 7–8
Private sector
  data protection in, 11–12
  Data Revolution, 2
  data systems features, 5–6
  innovation in, 38
  and public data, 10–11, 85, 122–123
  salaries, 109
  search platforms, 98
  and usefulness of data, 83
  workforce skills, 10
Programmatic agencies, 125–126
Protected Identification Keys (PIKs), 80
Public data. *See also* Data; Federal statistical system
  access to, 93–96, 103–105
  administrative, 88, 91, 111, 117–118
  bias in, 84
  confidentiality, 45, 60, 85
  costs, 5
  and democracy, 3–4, 87
  employer-employee, 88–91, 111
  function of, 1–2
  funding, 3
  importance of, 1
  and information, 11, 15
  infrastructure, 121, 141
  international comparisons, 23

and private sector, 10–11, 85, 122–123

and public policy, 4

quality, 5, 42

requirements of, 84–85

search platforms, 97–98

Public policy, 4

and data science, 120

and lower-income neighborhoods, 9

Putnam, George, 108, 113, 115, 118

Quarterly Workforce Indicators, 89, 115–116

Questions and Answers When Designing Surveys for Information Collections, 31

R&D laboratories, FFRDC, 132–133

Reagan, Ronald, 38, 46

Real GDP, 28–29

Reamer, Andrew, 53–54

Recommender engine, 101

Recovery.gov, 39

Reidentification, 93, 95–96

Reliability of data, 6–7

employment, 20–23

GDP, 19–22, 29–30

and measurement errors, 8–9

and privacy, 7–8

and rolling average approach, 9

Research

agricultural, 129–131

basic/applied, 70

funding, 68–70

reporting, 96–97

university R&D, 71, 80

ResearchGate platform, 101

Risk-scoring tool, 86–87

Romer, Paul, 65, 71

Ross, Wilbur, 36

Ryan, Paul, 116

Saez, Emmanuel, 59

Salaries, 109

Salvo, Joe, 83–84, 97, 101

Sampling, statistical, 33–34, 54–55

Saunders, Adam, 29

Schmalensee, Richard, 59

Science of Science and Innovation Policy (SciSIP) program, 75–76

Scientometrics, 72

Search platforms, 97–102

Semantic context of datasets, 100–101

Skill sets, data, 13–14, 118

Spending data, 44

StackOverflow, 102

Standards, national, 139–140

State agencies, 116, 120, 139

State Agricultural Experiment Stations (SAES), 130

Statistical agencies, 126–128

Statistical and Science Policy (SSP), 49–51

Statistics, public, 2. *See also* Federal statistical system; Public data

Statistics of Income Division of IRS, 128

STEM education, 80

Stiglitz, Joseph, 30

Stone, Richard, 25, 37, 57

Study and analysis centers, FFRDC, 133

Surveys, 31–37
  American Community Survey
    (ACS), 6–9
  Current Population Survey (CPS),
    20, 31–34
  data collection, 34
  data dissemination and protection,
    36
  errors, 35
  Federal Funds Survey, 68–69
  Federal Support Survey, 69–70
  National Longitudinal Survey of
    Youth 1997, 34–35
  reliability, 7
  sampling, 33–34
  steps in, 31–33
  weighting, 35
System engineering and integration
  centers, FFRDC, 133–134

Tagging datasets, 98
"Taking the Pulse of the Economy:
  Measuring GDP," 26
TANF Data Collaborative program,
  125
Taxation, military, 23–24
Tax data, unlawful disclosure of, 43
Training
  data skills, 117–120
  on-the-job, 88–89
Transaction data, 78–79

UK Research Excellence Framework,
  74–75
UMETRICS, 63, 66–67, 76–78, 98
Unemployment, 20, 22

Unemployment Insurance Wage
  Records, 115
Universities, 122
  academic centers, 124–125
  R&D, 71, 80
  and state agencies, 139
USDA, 52, 130
User engagement, 101–102
Utility/cost tradeoff, 87–88

Value of data, 96, 114–116
  and access, 103–105
  and automation, 102
  insiders and outsiders, 107–108,
    110–114
  and research outputs, 97

Waze, 9–10
Weiss, Roy, 75–76
Winchester, Simon, 4
Wissenschaftsrat, 56–57
Workforce boards, 89, 91, 113–116
Workforce capacity, 116–117, 120
Workforce churn, 89
Workforce Information Technology
  Support Center, 125–126
World War II, 26